AN AMERICA IN ANTIQUITY?

Mediterranean Perspectives: "La pensée de midi" and "Our Mezzogiorno"

LUCA MELDOLESI
A Colorni-Hirschman International Institute

Translated from Italian by Michael Gilmartin

BORDIGHERA PRESS
NEW YORK, NEW YORK

Il nostro mezzogiorno
Volume 1

Translated from Italian by Michael Gilmartin

This book series is dedicated to the presentation of new perspectives on how we might re-consider Southern Italy.

Cover Art: Pythagoras and Archimedes, detail from Raphael's *The School of Athens* in the Apostolic Palace, Vatican City, 1509–1511

ISBN 978-1-59954-207-2
Library of Congress Control Number: 2023951812

© 2024 Luca Meldolesi
All rights reserved,
Printed in the United States of America

BORDIGHERA PRESS
NEW YORK, NEW YORK

TABLE OF CONTENTS

INTRODUCTION ... 7

PART ONE • GENESIS
  CHAPTER 1 "The New Mediterranean Culture" ... 17
  CHAPTER 2 "A Plunge into the Archaic" ... 38
  CHAPTER 3 A Return Journey ... 65

PART TWO • FIGHTING BACK
  CHAPTER 4 European Pride, Mediterranean Pride ... 91
  CHAPTER 5 Get what I'm saying? ... 111

BIBLIOGRAPHY ... 137

INDEX OF NAMES ... 143

AUTHOR ... 147

When I left Calabria my frustration to get away was so great that I left in the middle of summer. I went to Bologna and attempted to study at DAMS [Drama, Art and Music Studies], but without success. Then to Paris, and finally I ended up in New York working as a photographer. I stayed there more than eight years. The irony is that only by escaping did I find out where I came from, who I was. Staying, for me, was like a rubber band that, once it had stretched to the edge of the world, flung me back again. It happened one day at the Met, the museum, among the Greek statues. The giant map at the entrance marked ancient Kroton—where some centuries later I would be born—as the center of Magna Graecia. I walked into that section as if under anesthesia. Someone, something from my past was looking for me. It was another me, I like to think, my double in fact, who through all those years of restless running had never given up following me.

Maurizio Fiorino (Crotone, 1984), photographer and writer
From "La Lettura," supplement to the *Corriere della Sera*,
11 September 2022

INTRODUCTION

1 — After seventy-seven years of planetary peace (albeit 'under arms' and marked by numerous local acts of war), the unexpected Russian invasion of Ukraine in February 2022 has put war in Europe back on the agenda, and with it the great danger of a Third World War.[1] This is a key issue which in my view should in a certain sense be traced to another and much broader human dimension.

The fact is that in our corner of the earth, the central Mediterranean, violence between human beings has surely been going on since time immemorial — between individuals, groups, tribes, affiliations, allies, peoples, etc.[2] But for a great deal of this time the pattern of conflictual rivalry that typically and systematically leads to stable vertical relationships of domination / subordination between whole populations did not yet exist.[3] Indeed, it only became firmly established during the rapid rise of Republican Rome and then in the quintessential Empire that followed. And it thus heralded — are we aware of this? — a bi-millennial nationalist-imperialist era,[4] one from which, sadly, we have not yet emerged!

To be more precise, starting with the end of the third and the beginning of the second millennium BC there was a historical period in the central Mediterranean during which numerous peoples, villages, and towns, 'armed one against the other' undertook self-promoting initiatives, both native and imported, which culminated in the so-called "Apennine culture" (Torelli 1984, 26), the apogee of the Etruscan and other native civilizations. Furthermore, there also existed an era of city-states

---

[1] I recall that in June-July 1943, writing from Melfi in Basilicata to Altiero Spinelli (now in Colorni 2019a, 159), Eugenio Colorni already feared such an eventuality should the forces producing these tragic upheavals not be brought under control by humanity — something which, despite enormous efforts, has clearly not yet been sufficiently achieved!
[2] As we shall see, this did not in any case impede the development, as early as the 5th to 4th millennium B.C. (Ross Holloway 1991, Chap. 1) the development of "an early trade network in obsidian, flint, alabaster, wool and manufactured goods between the coasts of southern Italy, Sicily, the Lipari Islands and Malta — allowing the latter to construct its extraordinary archaic temples" (Meldolesi 2007, 30). As for the 3rd and 2nd millennia, it is well known that there is a vast archaeological record bearing out the commercial influence of Cyprus, Crete and Mycenae in the central and western Mediterranean (Cf. below, n. 70).
[3] As had long been the case in the Eastern Mediterranean and Near East through the building of states, administrations, and imperial armed forces (Egyptian, Babylonian, Hittite, Assyrian, Persian). Cf. Liverani 1988, Meldolesi 2007, Chap. 1.
[4] Which brought us in the end to Kaisers and Tsars — that is, to the regimes of the Caesars.

and an accelerated civilizing process marked by extraordinary prosperity and colonization, a transition that only finally ended with the Punic Wars in the 3rd century BC.

It is a great story that is seldom discussed, but one that intrigues me. Because it shows how, initially, *it was possible to make concrete progress over a long period of time, outside the national-imperialist framework*, and how, at the same time, even when it was possible to live entire lifetimes outside this 'shirt of Nessus' that went on to reproduce itself over time in new forms, there still existed the danger of being attacked and overwhelmed — if there was no one able to master the situation and propel it on a different path.

Notwithstanding the fragility and brevity of human existence, these few observations might nevertheless be of interest to those who would like to "exert themselves" in looking for useful paths toward understanding how things *are*, how to act accordingly, and thus also how to prevent (as far as is humanly possible) these tragic recurring military disasters, which in addition aggravate endemic problems — social, natural, environmental, medical, and others as well. In other words, these opening remarks might be of interest to those who would like to venture slightly off the beaten path, aiming to gradually find a way into the Dante's open to 'gaze at the stars' — moving in the direction, that is, of the peaceful process of civilizing humankind.

These issues, doubts, and questions, those just mentioned, suddenly crowded into my head as I was setting up the present work. Not least because, to be useful, this work cannot simply be abstracted from one theoretical and practical Mediterranean experience — of my own and my ex-students and collaborators — which now spans forty years and has recently been presented in the numerous texts I have edited.[5]

Mine is, obviously, just one of many activities around the world that refer back to Albert Hirschman (starting with Europe, the United States and Latin America). These are mainly celebratory initiatives of generic cultural appeal. Some of them, however, are overseen by accomplished figures genuinely connected to the Hirschmanian legacy. And there is one that particularly interested me, so much so that of the

---

[5] AA.VV. 2018-22; Meldolesi 2020,2021; Meldolesi, ed., 2021, 2022. It cannot, moreover, be abstracted from the experience of our bilingual Colorni-Hirschman Institute (including, of course, its intensive editorial collaboration with four publishing houses (Peter Lang in Bern and New York, Bordighera New York, Rubbettino Soveria Mannelli, and Ide... Rome) nor from the "Harmonic Innovation Group" now under construction, a holding company for the incubation of open innovators with headquarters in Caraffa di Catanzaro.

pages that follow it gets 'the lion's share.'

I refer to the initiative in Marseilles spearheaded by Prof. Thierry Fabre, who nurtures a significant tradition of Mediterranean thought, and who at a certain point revealed a high level of agreement (a future expectation) with the viewpoint of Albert Hirschman. Like that of our own Mezzogiorno, it finds its roots in the fateful 1930s and the tragedy that followed.

It was thus that I found myself wishing to 'meet it halfway' by moving in an opposite direction. What I mean is, comparing our Colornian-Hirschmanian insights with "la pensée de midi" in the tradition of Gabriel Audisio and Albert Camus — in the hope of untangling along the way at least some of the difficult knots that bedevil us, briefly mentioned above...

2 — On the other hand, this volume is also part of the small series, mentioned above,[6] devoted to the critical re-examination of the theoretical-practical experience inspired by Albert Hirschman that I pursued at length in South Italy with numerous alumni and collaborators.

In the introduction to *Protagonismi mediterranei* [Mediterranean Protagonisms] (the most recent of these publications), in dialogue with Thierry Fabre's *Eloge de la pensée de midi* (Fabre 2007), I recalled how, during our journey, I myself and the people working with me had already encountered reasoning similar to what I later learned to call "la pensée de midi." In a sense, however, this had happened 'through an intermediary.'[7] Moreover, we had until then been unaware of the roots of this Algerian-Marseillan viewpoint. So that when I learned about it in Berlin, through my friend Wolf Lepenies, I was struck by its parallels with our own trajectory.

Sic stantibus rebus, I said to myself. Why not fathom the opportunity — and collaboration, perhaps — that might arise from a comparison of such experiences (with absolute mutual respect, of course, and with a view of potentially developing our discussion to other Mediterranean adventures that we can identify)?

In practical terms, it became clear that such a comparison requires a complex commitment. It can only be approached in stages, focusing

---

[6] Cf. n. 5.
[7] Meldolesi, ed., 2022. Cf. 19-24. I refer of course to Franco Cassano's *Pensiero meridiano* (1996) and to his Neapolitan friends: cf. in this regard A.A.V.V. 2020. As a result, I had the pleasant impression that our dialogue had already begun (albeit partially, improperly, unwittingly — that is, without our even knowing each other!).

attention, from one instance to the next, on specific aspects, epochs, and texts, and returning again and again to the selected (completed and examined) material from different viewpoints — until we can 'squeeze out' some at least of the lessons it inadvertently contains.[8]

Indeed, it struck me that the recent interest of Thierry Fabre and his 'circle' in Albert Hirschman's work might help us resume our inter-Mediterranean dialogue and even develop it substantially in pursuit of a credible perspective for the future. And that in any case, the contribution of "la pensée de midi" is important enough to permit a significant step forward on the overall problem that interests us. The fact that the progress of this *revived Mediterranean pride* is still partial in any case represents the possible beginnings of a further development — in the sense that it will have to be verified, completed, and even transformed in the light of further input from other shores.

And what is more, this first step (setting off on the 'right foot') is particularly important because it breaks the nationalist taboo on both the French and the Italian sides, and thus suggests similar solutions for other Mediterranean shores. It is precisely because of this that it must be crafted carefully, and in successive stages. And finally, I saw that, in order to facilitate such a *rencontre*, I would have to revisit (and rely on) some of my past work...

Of course, this is not a matter of restarting the line of reasoning *ab ovo*; nor is it a matter of reconstructing in detail a long-term (indeed, very long) problem. Basically, if I am to explain myself, I must focus my attention on a few carefully delimited issues and time frames.

So, after my introductory encounter with *Eloge de la pensée de midi* on the relationship between analysis and policy (contained in the introduction of *Protagonismi*), I thought I would continue the argument by taking a great leap backwards to 'assay' the foundations of the Marseille-Algerian current of thought. And to then ascend once again, following the footsteps of Albert Camus, back 'up the branches' towards us, though, inevitably, in a partial and provisional way.

My purpose is interactive.[9] My hope is that it may be of some use

---

[8] It may initially appear repetitive to return again and again to "the scene of the crime." But as I will try to show, it turns out to be indispensable if we are not to let go of the *ubi consistam* of the whole issue, which, if it is to materialize, needs to be discussed repeatedly and in depth.
[9] Through a series of "pairings": analysis-policy, past and present human history, long periods and individual events, etc. Tire reason is that, personally, I am willing to "side-step" what would ex-ante seem impossible in order to achieve the desired breakthrough. In this way I continue to respect "interpretive social science" (a la Rabinow and Sullivan, 1987), but I also

to our French counterparts (to southern and northern Mediterraneans, Africans, Middle Easterns, and European), and at the same time provide a better understanding of their arguments, not least in order to observe ours more critically — those, that is, of the 'veterans' of a Colornian- Hirschmanian scheme favoring South Italy — with the consequent intention of correcting its course (I, too, have reached the age of self-subversion!), readying its revival, and fostering its further trajectory (in terms of both reasoning and initiatives) in a broader Euro-African perspective.

3 — I will say, on the other hand, that the outcome — the one that matters (and, as with any self-respecting thriller, will emerge "fully fledged" only at the end of the story) — is particularly pleasing to me because it represents the culmination of a theoretical-practical thought process that began some time ago. This result is affected by a way of working that I adopted when I was young[10] and by the various phases of intense activity (educational, territorial, institutional, cultural, productive...) that my associates and I carried out collectively and at length in the Mezzogiorno.

Therefore, in order to help the reader untangle the meanderings

---

take exception to that view if it seems to me expedient to do so. For example: Eugenio Colorni, Albert Hirschman and Clifford Geertz did not appreciate 'history in the long run.' But to construct *Mediterranean Perspectives* I spontaneously used a sort of generalization from my 1992 *Il Ponte* article on Hirschman and Braudel. This was because I needed historical points of reference, long-term included, to be able to gradually 'spin out' my story about the present. Tire conclusion, therefore, in my view, is that we need to access pluralistic and flexible solutions that wholeheartedly respect factual reality, but also conform to the authors' intentions. (It is true on the other hand that a historical reconstruction of lines of thought is common to the three essays, "Linkages," "Exit-voice," and "Interest," that Albert Hirschman wrote for Tire New Palgrave Dictionary and are now in Hirschman 1986, just as it is true that Wolf Lepenies' work often makes use of a careful, cultural historian's reconstruction of the contributions of the authors under consideration.)

[10] A rebel from a good family looking *urbi et orbi* from the South for anyone who could help me understand where I had ended up (so that I could act), I found it useful to increasingly focus on the authors I intended to study seriously (such as Piero Sraffa and Joan Robinson) and their own key points of reference (such as David Ricardo and John M. Keynes). This gave rise later in my life to the sequence of intellectual protagonists who appear in the pages that follow, such as Fernand Braudel, Carlo Cattaneo, Albert Hirschman, Eugenio Colorni, Clifford Geertz, Gabriel Audisio, and Albert Camus. And to a way of working that acquires depth even as it loses breath with extension (and carries its own relative advantages and disadvantages). In fact, it comes across as alternative to those who, so to speak, dwell on the surface — perhaps 'on mainstream literature.' Yet it can be complementary to those who, starting with a very extensive bird's-eye view of knowledge (past and present, of many key texts and many different disciplines and cultures) are able to derive valuable analytical results. This was without a doubt a key to my "junior partnership" with Albert Hirschman.

of the unexpected encounter between "la pensée de midi" and "our Mezzogiorno" (the best-known formulations of the two respective experiences), it is worth setting out some initial points of reference.

Firstly, the posthumous dialogue with the two volumes of Gabriel Audisio's *Jeunesse de la Méditerranée* that opens the present work prompted me to 'dust off' a portion of what I had written at the time (in two volumes, *Il giuoco degli dei* [The Game of the Gods] and *Carlo Cattaneo e lo spirito italiano* [Carlo Cattaneo and the Italian Spirit]; Meldolesi 2006 and 2013a) about an archaic era in the central Mediterranean. I felt for various reasons that it was useful to give priority to the last prehistoric and the first historical period over other eras. Not because these others are less interesting or instructive but because the period cited takes us to the root of the civilizing process in our part of the world, which is what interests us most. Because just as in the case of individual human beings, youth put its 'imprint' on society, something that is undoubtedly transformed later but is never lost.[11] And in fact, during that beginning rapid and differentiated processes of indigenous civilizing took hold in our part of the world, fostered by the commercial and later colonial encounter with the East. This thus shows the existence of a 'city-state' period and archaic forms of federalism *prior* to the national-imperialist era which dominated human life from the rise of Rome on. And between the two periods there was an 'intermezzo,' in which the push for predominance (and the consequent subordination of others) prevailed — concretely represented by Syracuse and Carthage — *before* well and truly planting its roots in the last phase of republican Rome, soon to be transformed into the Empire.[12]

---

[11] Not by accident was Audisio's book called *Jeunesse de la Méditerranée* [Mediterranean Youth], a youth that, surprisingly, this "middle sea" always manages to renew... It is no coincidence that the curiosity that my *The Game of the Gods* was able to stimulate at the turn of the century among the young emerging tutors at the Prime Minister's Office represented an unexpected, immediate, and conversational verification of what I was trying to communicate about diversity, multi-identity, traditions, dormant potential, etc.

[12] By this I certainly do not mean to undervalue the role of Rome as home of the law (if for no other reason than since Nicoletta Stame and I are law graduates, we know something about it!) or the significant contributions of successive eras (the Renaissance and the Risorgimento come to mind). I wish only to emphasize the gap in continuity that exists between pre-Roman and Roman history, because otherwise there is a risk of losing sight of our own project. ("The interpretive key you provided is fundamental," Vincenzo Marino wrote to me in a private communication dated July 13, 2022, " — that is, to look for traces, signs and behaviors in the Mediterranean that shift the point of observation to cultures, identities, and conflicts that have stayed under the radar and that ought to be brought to light. The fact that 'history is written by the winners,' certainly hid an entire layer of knowledge, behaviors, and ways of life and thought that might represent the driving force behind a general perspective of global

This 'mirroring' of today's problems in that distant time interests me. Not in order to draw inspiration from it, 'just like that,' at so great a distance. But because — *repetita juvant* — it shows that there was an epoch of strong human ascendancy, certainly characterized by violence, localized warfare, and even endemic guerrilla warfare, but which nevertheless did not for any length of time adopt the pattern of domination/ subordination that became overwhelmingly entrenched later.[13]

There are in my view two important consequences of this. These are, first, that we need to know how to make the most of periods of peace, even the most temporary, to promote the civilizing of humanity and, second, that at the same time we should not delude ourselves. In order to avoid a return to the old ways, it is imperative to learn to pursue policies of distance reduction and the progressive mastery of dominance relations.

This is a decisive conclusion — even regarding theories of federalism. I say this in the sense that such institutional forms can indeed be valuable (at the Mediterranean, European, world level) provided we are able to act on the actual substance of human relations of subordination and toward the effective establishment of equal relations.

Third point. We now come to the modern era (and therefore to the second part of the present book). And we immediately realize that all this helps us enormously to understand our surroundings. If, moreover, with Camus (and Hirschman), we assign to *moderation* — and thus to nonviolent rebellion against injustice — a role as a starting engine for possible change, we find that we have constructed, at least in part, a useful tool for judging the positive and negative aspects of past experiences. And also, that we have at hand the beginning of a perspective that we must vigorously pursue if we are to begin to emerge from the national-imperialist impasse discussed above.[14]

In conclusion, the key requirement of Eugenio Colorni's politics

---

civilizing and pacification..." Too kind, dear Vincenzo, came to my mind. I would be happy, at least for now, to say that valuing and setting in motion that hidden reality might release an energy — direct and indirect — that will enable us to open a stretch of road leading the right direction. This in any case is my/our universalist proposal and the hope that keeps us going.)

[13] Not because the latter pattern was not already there in the bud — one should perhaps add. But because it was being held temporarily in check by the pushes and counter-pushes of the forces in the field.

[14] It is an achievement, this, that belongs to many mothers and fathers, such as those mentioned above in n. 10. But it emerges concretely, not only from meeting with them, but from practice — from what, as we shall see, is leading us today to undertake private innovative construction, but in the public interest.

thus finds new life and can be theorized and put into practice concretely, including through much trial and error. This is one of the decisive fields my friends and I are concretely involved in....

Agerola, August 2022

PART ONE
GENESIS

CHAPTER 1

"The New Mediterranean Culture"

To get the navigation of the present work started, I would like to propose a recurring personal question of mine, though from a somewhat different vantage point. Namely, does it make sense to bring together multiple texts, multiple aspects, and multiple epochs for the purpose of gradually probing broad issues such as the Mediterranean perspective that interests us here? My answer is positive, provided that before embarking on such an adventure, we can at least glimpse a common thread in the sea of reference material.

This is what I will try to show in the pages that follow, beginning (first of all) with two books from 1935-36 by Gabriel Audisio and a famous 1937 inaugural lecture by Albert Camus for the opening of the new "Maison de la culture" in Algiers — while keeping in mind at the same time the evolved contemporary version of the issue as contained in the *Eloge de la pensée de midi* by Thierry Fabre. [15]

I believe (though it may be an illusion) that by grasping (as far as possible) 'the extreme endpoints' of that point of view, it will be easier to compare them later to certain pertinent references to them, identified with the help of additional texts. (Cf. Part Two of this book). In doing so, I think it will become easier to compare such 'highs and lows' with my own and my collaborators' experience.

Specifically, that is, with what I wrote following the tragedy unleashed in 2001 by international Islamic terrorism (referred to in the United States by the abbreviation "9/11") — including its much-feared consequences, which unfortunately have since come to pass.[16] And then comparing them with a judgment on the current Russian invasion of Ukraine — barbaric, inhumane, highly destructive — which has reminded us of the great danger of world war (right down to the nuclear threat that could even lead to the extinction of humankind).[17]

From all this I would draw some preliminary questions. Firstly,

---

[15] Fabre 2007 — cf., above, sec. 2 of the "Introduction."
[16] Cf. below, par. 12 in Ch. 2.
[17] This of course alongside the need to actually protect health, life, education, freedoms, the environment — first and foremost with respect to fossil-based energies — a 'must' of which, thanks to the urging of the younger generation, we are becoming increasingly aware.

after millennia of violence, nationalism, and imperialism, is it possible to glimpse in the long-term fortunes of this ancient basin of humanity that is the Mediterranean a possible *emergency exit*?[18]

And in addition, beginning with some contemporary watersheds like those just mentioned (the years before the Second World War, the rise of Islamic-inspired terrorism and the dangerous redefining of some of the global imbalances in which we find ourselves),[19] would a current re-proposition of "la pensée de midi," expanded and rounded out in a Colornian-Hirschmanian approach, be potentially fertile and promising?

And again, how to embark (if it is even possible) on the path we are looking for? What characteristics should it possess to convince us that we have identified it and are really 'on the right track'?

Of course, these are painful, bold, impertinent, perhaps provocative questions, supported by a still meager itinerary that will most likely need to be supplemented later by additional texts, eras, and perspectives.

But they do suggest a focus on the numerous difficulties and potentials that arise from the desired rapprochement — and the lessons to be learned from it — between two curiously parallel Mediterranean experiences[20] (those, namely, of "la pensée de midi" [21] and of "our

---

[18] I have borrowed this famous title from Ignazio Silone (1965) to allude to a critical problem in my "ruminating": is it possible to escape from the nationalist and imperialist vertical structure of the world system that has "n" dimensions in order to progress further on the path of freedom, democracy, fraternity, social justice, gender, beauty, peace, welfare, respect for nature? How?

[19] These three clearly negative turning points have perhaps generated (or are producing or could produce) reactions that represent important developments in thought. They could be set alongside other, perhaps positive ones — such as victory in the World War or the fall of the Berlin Wall — which, however, in practice seem to have had less clear, less disruptive effects (so much less as to suggest that peoples' creative responsiveness is greater in the face of danger than with respect to success a subject beyond the scope of this essay). However, in either case, my intention is to introduce into the social-political sphere Albert Hirschman's (1958, 1986) well- known economic thesis on the *tipping point* as a "releaser" of energy. Are we able to understand and learn to harness, in the interest of the inhabitants of our planet, the many manifestations of creativity and vitality in the various spheres of life — i.e., the very numerous "boraciferous blowholes" that surround us? Hic Rhodus!

[20] They both began in the mid-1930s (first in Algiers and then in Trieste) and, by way of (sometimes) labyrinthine adventures, they continue to this day.

[21] This is the title of the last chapter of *L'homme révolté [The Rebel]* — a well-known philosophical-political text by Albert Camus (1951). On the other hand (as we shall see in Part Two of this book) "la pensée de midi" represents — albeit with some discrepancies — the poetic-literary version of the same order of problems.

Mezzogiorno"[22]) in such a way as to finally allow (this is my idea) some useful theoretical-practical conclusions to be drawn.

I

1 — I would therefore like to begin with "la pensée de midi" in the 1930s, before the expression was coined. For this purpose, however, it is first necessary to unravel a knot that tends to recur with respect to the texts concerned. I refer to authors with a philosophical-literary background. Each of their individual writings in a certain sense represents a unique theoretical and artistic exemplar. Consequently, the social scientist who, from his or her own perspective, seeks to verify their contribution (and perhaps the consequences it may have for his or her own work) must guard against minimizing their achievements (which will have to be carefully 'extracted' from the narrative and/or identified to one side). But care must also be taken to guard against an overestimation of their claims — something that would inevitably result from a hasty scrutiny of the texts. Ours is actually a third way, which, as we shall see, turns out to be rather circuitous in practice and, precisely for this reason, needs to be built carefully...

Generally, the origin of "the new Mediterranean culture" (aka "la pensée de midi") is traced to the so-called "Algiers group," composed of Jean Grenier, Gabriel Audisio, and Albert Camus, who later became its most prominent exponent, and, as well, its *aoidos*.

In fact, Jean Grenier, philosopher and man of letters,[23] formerly a lecturer at the Institut Français in Naples, moved to Algiers, where he had a brilliant pupil, Albert Camus, who went on to have a dazzling career (that included a Nobel Prize).

Camus was born in Algeria, at Mondovi (now Dean) in 1913, into a poor family, and never even knew his father (a farm worker and French settler, who died in the Great War). Between Jean Grenier and Albert Camus an intimate friendship was forged that was destined to last, despite their differing practical orientations — contemplative the former, militant the latter.

A third exponent of this "new culture" was Gabriel Audisio. Born in Marseilles at the beginning of the last century into a family of stage artists, he moved to Algiers because his father, Piedmontese by birth,

---

[22] Cf. the relevant webinar on the site www.effeddi.it.
[23] Cf. for example, Grenier 1933 and 1959 for the literary side, 1961 for his philosophy.

had become director of that city's opera house. He had studied, Gabriel, at the French school in Algiers (with additional courses in literature, law and Muslim civilization). After furthering his education at Science Po in Paris and taking part in the Great War as a volunteer, Audisio had returned to Algeria to compete for the post of Rédacteur de Préfecture, which he won.

Assigned initially to the Prefecture of Constantine, Gabriel later became general Rédacteur of the Government. On the side, he had meanwhile taken up literature and poetry — even before his journey led him to Grenier and Camus. Perhaps as a reaction to the bureaucratic environment he found himself in (and aided as he was by frequent business trips to Algeria that allowed him to gauge its pulse with respect to metropolitan France), he wrote two important volumes on his experiences in the mid-1930s, *Jeunesse de la Méditerranée I* and *II*.

It is worth looking at these more closely.

We can begin with the contents of the first book. The six chapters that follow the introduction sketch out an itinerary by sea from his native Marseille to Algiers, Morocco, Spain, Tunisia, the Tyrrhenian Sea, the Balearics, and the Tuscan islands.[24] It is an account of multiple Mediterranean voyages that stops at the Sicilian Channel, not venturing even into the Ionian Sea, the Adriatic, or the Aegean, much less beyond. It deals only with the western Mediterranean. [25]

But Audisio thinks all this is enough for him to speak of the Mediterranean as a whole. So that early in the introduction to the volume, *Mediterranean Homeland,* [26]- he draws in advance a number of general conclusions from these journeys that are at once marine, terrestrial, climatic, cultural, psychological, etc.

For example, he argues (making some unexpected claims we will have to come back to) that "the many successive dominant powers are but 'moments,' transitory aspects of the eternal Mediterranean," and that while "nations pass away, the substance of countries remains"

---

[24] It is a path that surely corresponds to the author's own explorations and is proposed from within French culture, which was then predominant in the Western Mediterranean not least because Algeria, Morocco and Tunisia were at the time colonies of France.
[25] "Undoubtedly," Audisio writes further on (1935, 135), "I have practiced my trawling only on the seabed of the Western part of the Mediterranean, but I do not despair of reinforcing the experience by reaching the antipodes, little by little." However, in a note he adds," what is true for one [part of the Mediterranean], is often true for the other. I am well aware that there are still the Adriatic, the Levantine Sea, the Aegean, the archipelagos... Moorings need to be reserved" in order to explore them.
[26] This is followed by a second part, *Nautical Instructions,* informative in character.

(Audisio 1935,12 e 17).[27] The Mediterranean, he adds, is not part of Europe — it is 'the sixth part of the world,' 'a kind of liquid continent with solidified borders,' 'a homeland.' And he doesn't stop there. "I believe in the unity of the Mediterranean"; "The Mediterranean has often divided its coastal areas, but it has never separated them";[28] "'resemblances among friends' are the great law of the Mediterranean, from one shore to the other, and anything that divides, you can be sure, is only a sign of exquisite subtleties in an eternal kinship"; "the truth is that the Mediterranean should form only one maritime 'nation,' and it should have not one capital, but ten — all the great ports with their respective charters, elevated to 'free cities,' with peoples and languages intermingled."[29]

"I know and I repeat," Audisio continues, "that Mediterranean countries have always been meant to join one another as naturally as the vine joins the olive tree. It took our modern sense of nationality, and its insane contemporary glorification, to appear to break this spell," which — the author seems to suggest implicitly — ought to be revived.[30] But how? This is indeed a key question, one that hangs like a sword of Damocles over my incipient reasoning....

2 — For a French state official who — we should not forget — published his *Jeunesse de la Méditerranée* after Hitler's accession to power, and who was therefore (in all likelihood) doggedly searching for an intellectual alternative to the current way of thinking at a time when very black clouds were gathering over our part of the world,[31] this was

---

[27] These are extreme, indisputable statements, that hint — as we shall see further on — at a relationship between past and present to be developed further.
[28] Charles-Roux, 1931,10. Similarly: "Well before the Aegeans and Phoenicians... the Mediterranean... united rather than separated" — Hérubel 1928,19; "in no age was the Mediterranean a barrier" — Benoît 1931,3. (See Audisio 1935,14,15,16).
[29] Ibid.16, 18. "With its international status," the passage continues, "Tangier should give you an idea of this — where you are answered in Spanish when you speak French, or in Arabic when you speak Italian." It is, moreover, not at all foreign, Audisio adds in a note, since "there has existed since 1928 a Conference of French Chambers of Commerce of the Mediterranean Basin that groups 49 consular assemblies, from Spain to Egypt, from Algeria to Greece." Of course, "it's not foreign at all," I feel like commenting, but France-centric without a doubt...
[30] I find this passage (from ibid. 21) illuminating. Evidently it was the tragic epoch then looming that suggested to Audisio the start of a quest which, however, to make real sense — this is my impression — would require extraordinary persistence and dedication.
[31] "Even if I were on my own," Audisio wrote, for example, in the second volume of *Jeunesse* (1936,95-6), "I would continue to protest, to be honest. It is not a matter of knowing if I think I'm the only one who knows the truth, but [of knowing] to what extent each person remains true to his or her thoughts. Let us avoid confusion. We live in a time when everyone must

doubtless a daydream, a spreading of wings, a bold claim, "a feat of imagination" that still arouses surprise and admiration in our minds today — not least because, as we shall see later, it unveils a way of thinking (and a long-term perspective) that we Mediterraneans, though instinctively familiar with one another, do not generally have the audacity to bring into focus....

And there is more. These ideas began to take shape in Algiers at the same time as a similar tenacious search for alternatives (and perspectives) by Eugenio Colorni and the very young Albert Hirschman in Trieste (Meldolesi 2013, Chap. 2), another important Mediterranean port (albeit outside the area explored by Audisio). And the fact that his thinking along with that of Camus and Grenier, later resulted in "la pensée de midi," while in the same time frame, Colorni, the Hirschmann siblings and Spinelli were conceiving the goal of European unity, inevitably suggests to me a hypothesis that I would like to test. This is that these two "visions" are compatible and can be seen as two faces of own much-desired future. This is another lingering question that will keep the reader company through the following pages.

On the other hand, it is not easy to approach a critical analysis of the first volume of *Jeunesse de la Méditerranée*. Indeed, its long excursus touches on a thousand key aspects of the Mediterranean condition, undertaking an objective and subjective reconnaissance that sometimes leads to a celebration. How to take in its many analytical and propositional aspects, I asked myself, without being captured by its literary seductions?

We must proceed point by point — this is my answer — successively specifying the purpose of each, cutting the analysis as we see fit, and delimiting the space-time horizon as we go along.

As it happens in fact, commenting on the viewpoint that emerges in Algiers in Thierry Fabre's contemporary interpretation, I have argued[32] that in order to be set in motion, the Mediterranean pride and ambition to be awakened must take account of the limitations and open problems in the cultural and material condition of the peoples gravitating to the "middle sea" — something that, together with numerous

---

take a stand, when everything matters, when all words carry purpose, when all gestures are deadly or salutary. No ambiguity. I refuse to base my friendships on reticence — making my own frank examination of conscience matters more to me than exposing myself to reprisals." This is a significant statement — it hints at an underlying intellectual restlessness, like the calm before the storm.

[32] Meldolesi ed., 2022, Introduction.

alumni and collaborators, I have long tried to argue with regard to the Italian Mezzogiorno.

Now, however, I want to move in the opposite direction. I would like to ask what the point of view expressed in *Jeunesse de la Méditerranée* would suggest for my work in terms of corrections and further developments.

3 — A first step along these lines, I would say, has already been taken. It concerns the need to break out of the shell of mainstream life (local, southern, national, European) and actually venture into the Mediterranean as it is, with its plurality of societies, languages, cultures — and with important consequences in terms of reorientation.[33]

But other indications undoubtedly exist as well, and I hope they will come to the surface in stages as we continue reading *Jeunesse*.

Already in "People of the South," the second section of the first chapter "Territory of Marseille," Audisio questions what it is that wealthy civilized people from the north come to the Mediterranean to do. His answer, of course, is that they come to restore themselves, to be rejuvenated. But is it just *joie de vivre* (and perhaps to die and be buried in the sun in one of the many cemeteries on the coast)? "Goethe and especially Nietzsche," the author responds, "taught the southern journey to their peers: If you can steer the vessels of your desires to the southern shores, the happy islands...' How nostalgic!" (Audisio 1935, 52).

It isn't just the physical climate. It is a social, moral, and perhaps philosophical climate that they are looking for. This is because in reality it concerns "the eternal and practical problems of our existence — daily well-being and the quiet heroism of holding on to the [human] measure of a perfectly human universe. Living *well* and dying *well*."

And later: "peoples born from the Mediterranean, burdened by centuries and civilizations, are always able to come back and be green again, like the laurel near a spring." "This is the lesson that needs to be learned" (Ibid. 1935, 52, 53).

Except that, dazzled by (and in love with) such a seductive image, Audisio mutes every other issue to the point of exclaiming, "For you [people of the Midi], poverty is nothing more than an absence of personal possessions, for which resentment and jealousy are absent. Adversity leaves you confident, misfortune finds you dignified. The laughter and health, the chimera and fantasy which you possess in

---

[33] Beginning with my *Il giuoco degli dei:* cf. below, Chap. 2.

such profusion, I need not lay claim to, for I carry them with me. But to your wisdom, to your teaching I would return without fail."[34]

II

4 — As we can see,[35] Audisio here subscribes to a fundamentally static (albeit attractive), even millennarian, descriptive view, observed from the outside with respect to most of the flesh-and-blood inhabitants of the Mediterranean. He doesn't even raise the question (which must inevitably play a central role from a policy perspective) of appealing to Mediterraneans themselves regarding the goals of development and democracy. That is, aiming to enhance the positive aspects and neutralize (or combat) the negative aspects of their condition in order to abolish misery and jointly present a credible alternative to what passes for modernity (the winds of war included, of course).

So, from this point of view our roads diverge (as we shall see below). But this does not erase what Audisio had the courage to argue on the positive side of the Mediterranean issue. If anything, it suggests that we follow his itinerary step by step, reserving the right to review it later, critically — at the most appropriate time...

Clearly, however, this will not amount to offering the reader a concise account of Audisio's nautical and cultural explorations. It is instead possible to read the book *with a purpose in mind,* looking for a common thread suggested perhaps by the complexity of the subject matter and subsequent history.

Indeed, this was the case in my own reconnaissance. In scrolling through the volume, I was driven above all by curiosity — to discover how the author would 'manage' in dealing with the great historical wound that still largely divides the two main shores of the Mediterranean. I speak of the contrast between the Western culture of Greco-Roman origin and the Eastern culture of Jewish-Semitic (and therefore also Phoenician-Punic-Arab-Muslim) origin. Is it enough — I wondered — to argue that "the Mediterranean has often divided its coastal areas, but it has never separated them"?[36]

---

[34] Audisio 1935, 58-9. To the point of quoting Pliny (on 54) regarding life for a Southerner: "Nothing more miserable and nothing prouder. For in his treasury is the knowledge of his miseries and the judgment of his pride."
[35] As glimpsed in the Introduction: cf. above, secs. 1 and 2.
[36] Audisio 1935, 15 (and, above, sec. 1).

"For many centuries," Audisio replies at one point, referring to Algeria,[37] "Rome shaped this country, and for many more centuries it was shaped by Islam: there is the arch of Trajan and the mosque of Sidi-bou-Médiene. The heart always sways between one and the other. Perhaps the truth is very much *(extremement)* between the two."

The author is thus without doubt aware that he is searching for a precarious balance (or rather a perpetually shifting imbalance), a "midpoint" that is constantly being redefined.[38] And having personally come from Marseilles, it is to his credit that he made an effort to carefully observe the situation "in reverse" with respect to France. That is to say, from the opposite coast of the Mediterranean. In the third chapter, "Crossing from Morocco and Spanish color," for example, we read (Audisio 1935,117 and 118) that "many years in the Maghreb have given me an African soul. At the moment of [...] crossing from the lands of Islam to Christian Europe, I am compelled to conjure up the Saracen ancestors!"

"For me – he continues - it is not that the Spain of the *remontada was* Africa, but that it *still is.* And do you know where it stops? The Spanish journey ought to be undertaken, rather, by descending to the Midi, to the palm trees, to the sort of end of the world that is Andalusia. I [instead] will go and see where the north begins..."

Here, clearly, the intention to bring the two shores of the Mediterranean as close as possible merges and melts into personal experience.

It is a theme that reappears many times in the book in other contexts. For example, in the fourth chapter, "From Tunis to the Italian Tyrrhenian," Audisio writes (1935,143), "in Naples I had the choice — either Greek Sicily or peasant Sardinia. I chose Sardinia. There is a sort of barbarian in me who rejoices in boarding a 'tub' bound for this destination without prestige: Cagliari. But perhaps the pseudo-barbarian has some secret motives. First of all, the attraction of a modest port. Small Mediterranean ports!" Like those in Sardinia, obviously— long influenced by Phoenician-Punic nautical culture (194).

This impression comes across even more sharply in the fifth chapter, "Balearic necklace," especially when we read (ivi), "the many similarities that the Balearics display with North Africa is not at all surprising when we recall that a large proportion of Algerian settlers

---

[37] Ibid., 106.
[38] Which of course suggests the idea of the Mediterranean as a middle sea, well suited to mediate between different points of view...

originated from these islands. The exchange between communicating vessels took place so smoothly that it is not known whether it is Palma that owes Bab-el-Oued its arcade market or Bab-el-Oued that owes Palma its lafatieri and anisette."

Or in the sixth chapter, "Small port on the Tuscan sea," when, speaking of Corsica, Audisio writes, "these houses made of stacked shale slabs, adjoining each other, with covered passages, vaults, stairs, zigzagging lanes, these defensive piles against man, nature and beasts, these rocky agglomerations overlooking a sea of pirates and the valleys of invaders, Nonza, Pino, Corte — this is Africa, it is Kabilya" (228).

5 — The landscape where Audisio's fascinating exposition unfolds, however, is fundamentally 'French.' In fact, in its literary sweep (which may talk about locations, the sea, fish, birds, goddesses, myths, culture, etc.) this perception is repeatedly felt. The few observations that concern the Berber and Arab populations (and, indeed, the Spanish or Italian ones as well) are intermittent and mostly experienced from the outside. It is clear that they are not part of his personal pursuits.

This leads me to return to the discussion of the book's general approach (mentioned above at the beginning of sec. 1). Hirschman invites us to consider literature as a source for our work. Which means that its contributions, from the point of view of the social scientist (rather than the person of letters), must be carefully sifted and inevitably placed in a different context.[39]

---

[39] Not least because the social scientist has an obligation of scientific honesty (Colorni would say sincerity) toward his or her own work that does not belong in "fine literature." With respect to the first volume of *Jeunesse* (and in particular to what has been discussed so far) I have learned that in order to talk about the Mediterranean as such, it is necessary to cross the boundaries of one's own area (and country), to build on experience, and also to take an active interest in the affairs of other Mediterranean peoples, especially those most different from our own. In this regard, we must base our beliefs on doubt, evaluation and careful verification, and proceed cautiously by gradual processes of generalization. For example, we must put forward general theses — such as, for example, that of the Mediterranean homeland — simply as hypotheses (however important) awaiting findings. In addition, it is necessary to capture the many alluring aspects of this sea (often described in literature) and the peoples who inhabit its shores. But as I have mentioned, it is also essential to take on board their difficulties as well as their achievements, specifying in each case (often in new ways and forms) what we intend to leant and construct. We must be constantly aware of the limits of our own research and must learn in parallel from those of others, especially Mediterraneans, assessing their compatibility. For example, once the respective value of the two experiences (that is, "la pensée de midi" and the Colornian-Hirschmanian experience of "our Mezzogiorno") has been recognized, it will be possible to proceed to a closer dialogue, and to attempt at partial comparisons that nevertheless respect each other's absolute independence, etc. A fruitful relationship can thus be created, open to other possible inputs,

This would be an intense intellectual labor (like a craftsman's), one that might arise from experience and from reading some attractive texts, such as the first volume of Gabriel Audisio's *Jeunesse de la Méditerranée*. It is a project which, to achieve good results, would have to be nurtured by further learning — for example, via the second volume of *Jeunesse*, to which we shall now turn our attention. It is a text that has an evocative title *Sel de la mer* [Salt of the sea] along with a warning: "this book was born out of an opportunity: the author was invited to visit Tunisia, to see, hear and say what he *felt, freely*" (Audisio 1936, 9).[40]

So that while the first book of *Jeunesse* was composed little by little beginning in the late 1920s, the second was written on the spur of the moment, as a follow-up to the first, as if to reinforce its intellectual and political message.

Indeed, from the very first pages, the scene is bursting with the French settler's irrepressible nostalgia for Africa, the memories of his long-gone youth, the characteristics of places and civilizations, and with them the climate, the plant, animal and sea life, etc.

Why, I wonder, after so much water has passed under the bridge, when the enchantment Audisio sought to evoke in this volume is now *révolu à jamais*-[41] - why do I feel the need to understand *how* an intellectual, French civil servant could return to his roots in a Tunisia "bathed in the waters of memory" — in the mid-1930s?[42]

The answer is simply because it seems useful for my purposes. I am trying to build an intellectual path that sets out on the road to a new Mediterranean culture (also desired, as we shall see, by Albert Camus). And above all because this volume by Audisio without a doubt contains a cultural breakthrough that particularly interests me.

In fact, utilizing Tunisian archaeological sites and their reuse in current life as an introductory expedient,[43] Audisio superbly evokes a

---

which can be consolidated over time.
[40] "Opportunity," he continues, "is a good thing when it is the straw that breaks the camel's back: the author was only begging it to break. Opportunity also makes a man a thief — the author also found Tunisia bathed in the waters of remembrance, where he surreptitiously fished out all his fish."
[41] That is to say, after decolonization and the Algerian war, and after Marseilles, long a sociopolitical bastion of the so-called *pieds-noirs*, finally turned the page.
[42] Cf. above, n. 40.
[43] "To make the ruins come alive," Audisio writes at one point (1936, 37-8), "I need Mr. Cucurello, his country's trinket peddler, chauffeur in his spare time, and also consular agent of the Kingdom of Italy, who drives me from Teboursouk to Degga while recounting the Mussolini legend — 'This Mussolini is cunning, *cunning, goddammit!*'"

famous ancient clash that we might want to take a cue from in looking for new Mediterranean trajectories: the confrontation between Rome and Carthage. (From which sprang, of course, the historical events we know so well — including the many nationalisms and Holy Roman Empires... both past and present).

Remember Cato the Censor's famous *"Delenda est Carthago"*?[44]

III

6 — "No place has been more severely judged than Carthage,"[45] wrote Audisio, opening the chapter "The Salt of Carthage," "or to put it better: no place has been more slandered than Carthage." It is clear from this beginning that the author's argument is above all cultural.

The passage in fact continues: "The prejudices that have been dragged around everywhere are well known. Writers, essayists, and historians have delighted in accumulating characteristics that put a hateful face on the Punic city. One must therefore plunge the grappling hook into that pile: from the reshuffled outrages justice may come forth, and from this ancient story a living lesson may emerge."

This, then, is the central purpose of the book. Writers, essayists, and historians have left us an image of Carthage that is intolerable, outrageous, constructed for the use and consumption of the victors. Audisio intends to turn that portrait upside down to do justice to the defeated. Agreed — it is an important breakthrough, perhaps crucial (this will emerge more clearly below). But to be able to make such a judgment, I would first need to know how things played out at the concrete, historical level.[46]

In the next chapter, I will therefore take the liberty of setting the Audisian excursus (which I present here in its briefest essence) alongside some lessons from Carlo Cattaneo and from *Memory and the Mediterranean*[47] by Fernand Braudel, the great French historian whom I

---

[44] As Braudel wrote (1998, 242): "Who in their heart — and historians, even impartial ones, have a heart — did not mourn over old Cato's 'Delenda est Carthago,' and the ruthless destruction ordered by Scipio Aemilianus? A most original voice was thus condemned to silence."
[45] In the third section of the first chapter of *Jeunesse II, Sel de la mer*, 47.
[46] This is more than understandable if the purpose is not merely descriptive or polemical. Because in the present work we would also like to find inspiration to explore exit routes out of our (imaginable) present difficulties. Is this not so?
[47] It is a book written "almost off the cuff, and with great pleasure" in 1968-70 and published in France and Italy in 1998, edited by R. de Ayala and P. Braudel, with a preface and notes by J. Guilaine and P. Rouillard.

had the pleasure of meeting. Conceived (also almost spur-of-the-moment) more than 30 years after Audisio's two books, this posthumous volume was a reference text for my own *The Game of Gods*. And so it makes sense, even just out of curiosity, to do a rapid textual comparison between what I had written, some of Braudel's pages, and the second book of *Jeunesse*, arriving (as we shall see) at the conclusion that, surprisingly, *Sel de la mer* "holds up" quite well in its central message (even though, to be truly convincing, it needs further qualifications).

In the first place, keeping in mind the atmosphere of the time,[48] we immediately see why Audisio holds that the true "crime" imputed retrospectively to Carthage is that it was a Semitic and Jewish city, even as regards its origin.[49] "Of the perpetual conflict that exists," he writes, between East and West, "I am well aware. The Mediterranean has two basins: the eastern and the western — the sea of sunset and the sea of dawn. Two geographical poles, two spiritual poles. Contact between them sends up sparks down the centuries. [...] But the sparks also show that a current can exist and circulate between the two poles. [...] The location of Tunis is a sensitive place, at the very center, at the heart of the Mediterranean. It is something like the precise point on which the weighing arm of a scale rests" (Audisio 1936, 51-2).

And so, I note, the setting of the second volume of *Jeunesse de la Méditerranée* is different from that of the first. The initial western (and French) bias is now replaced by a "balance" point located in the central Mediterranean — a question that obviously also closely affects the Mezzogiorno in our country.

The book proceeds with a brief discussion of Carthaginian civilization (and the lies that have beset it *in saecula saeculorum)*, which in the end leads the author to argue that the culture of Carthage (material and spiritual, popular and learned) is still present "everywhere."[50]

---

[48] Cf. above, secs 1 and 5; and nn. 30, 31 and 43.
[49] "What we know of the history of Tyre and the rest of Phoenicia before the eighth century," writes Warmington (1968, 19; cf. also 80) "comes mostly from the Old Testament and from Assyrian Records. The best-known circumstance is the alliance between Hiram of Tyre (c. 969-936) and King Solomon, and there were close relations between Tyre and the Israelites for the next two centuries [decisive for the Phoenician discovery of the western Mediterranean]." Braudel writes (1998, 202-03) that the Phoenicians were "friends or indeed allies [of the Jews]. It was Phoenicians from Tyre who had built the temple and royal palace in Jerusalem in the age of Solomon (c. 970-930), and Phoenician boats which had sailed on behalf of the Jewish king to Ophir (in southern Arabia or India?) [...]; it was again Phoenician craftsmen building in the city of Ezion-Geber, who had built large metal-working furnaces for smelting copper and iron, by far the most advanced in the ancient world, according to W.F. Albright."
[50] In religion, in names, in culture, in architecture, in toponymy, in irrigation, in cultivation,

Hence the invective, noted above, against Rome (represented at the time by Mussolini). At first the philippic seems almost absurd. "Scorn the ruins?" he asks, for example, in the first chapter of *Sel de la mer* (Audisio 1936, 32). "I would say rather that I detest them, particularly the Roman ones."

Later, however, the reasoning broadens, both on a personal and political-cultural level. "As far as I can go back in my memory," he writes, "I always find myself *against* Rome, and on the side of its enemies, its victims, standing with those Rome has defeated. I do not make this observation without sadness, after so willingly crowing about what the Mediterranean can do — its harmony, its unity. Rome cannot be discounted, that is certain. But paradoxical as this may seem, I see Rome in the music of the Mediterranean as musicians once saw the tritone: the devil, discord. *Diabulus in musica*" (Audisio 1936, 91).

And further on: "I would therefore like to be properly understood. There is no question in my mind of suppressing Rome, the Latin civilization, and its historical role, nor of excluding it from the Mediterranean. *The point is to protest against the abuse of it, against the excessive space accorded to it.* On behalf of the Mediterranean and of Mediterranean genius I stand up against the exclusive worship of Rome, because Rome is perhaps the thing the Mediterranean has produced that is least Mediterranean. My aim is to put Rome 'back in its place,' which is no doubt eminent but is neither the summit nor the whole." "The world does not begin and end with Rome. Neither does the Mediterranean. And the Mediterranean is not Rome."

"No doubt ancient Rome achieved one of the unifications of the Mediterranean — evident and prolonged. But this in no way proves that this embodied its genius, it only proves that Rome's enterprise of hegemony was successful. In a case like this I don't think success is the criterion of moral worth [do you]? And yet that is precisely where Rome's disciples are leading us — to the worship of force and success

---

etc., to the point of sometimes crossing the line, it must be added, into myth. For example, at the end of the first volume of *Jeunesse* [1935, 208], Audisio quotes Lucian: "in Phoenicia I see the statue of the goddess Derkéto: a strange spectacle because, though half-woman, starting from the thighs it ends in a fish tail"; and then Pausanias: "at Figalia one sees a temple of Eurynomé, whose statue, woman to the thighs, ends as a fish"; and then comments: "I see in these siren myths more than the survival of ancestral totemism. I see an image of what we may have been in a previous life [...]. I believe in an original identity of man and beast, of which the goddess Derkéto and the statue of Eurynome preserve for us testimony. Hie memory comes back to us even at the end of our lives. Have I not also happened to feel like a bird?" (For the history of Carthage, see Warmington 1968).

through force" (Audisio 1936, 104).[51]

7 — Exactly! To summarize in a nutshell this provisional (subjective and cross-sectional) foray of mine into the two volumes of *Jeunesse de la Méditerranée*, I would emphasize the following points.
With regard to certain historical events, there is a great need to think anew, with a fresh mind, sincerely and without pretenses. It is prompted first and foremost by the arrival of a negative historical turning point[52] — like the precursors of World War II, 9/11 in 2001 with respect to Islamist terrorism, the current Russian invasion of Ukraine.

Building on such tragic experiences, it is imperative to point the finger at 'the worship of force and success through force.' This is, in essence, the cultural lesson from Audisio that we must actively and untiringly promote.

We need to ground this issue in concrete historical foundations, even distant ones — to develop an awareness of it, certainly, but also to enable us to search for a possible livable alternative to the worrying state of affairs we now find ourselves in on a daily basis.

All this, in turn, requires new research aimed at 'understanding more about it,' at identifying the characteristics and theoretical-practical rationale of the new Mediterranean culture we are trying to address.

We must be aware, however, that this is only a starting point, a quiet suggestion (to those who feel up to it) to progress further in theory and practice — methodically,[53] steadily, and quickly.

For now, we must be content with Audisio's (attractive, but unfortunately utopian) re-proposal of the Mediterranean homeland: "a unity [...] founded on community of thought and respect for human truths, a Mediterranean homeland made for the soul of an international community of peoples of the sea, offered as an example to the world and to all other human families in their widest *rassemblements*. Utopia, if you will. But the utopia of today is the oxygen of the future. And I believe in the future of the Mediterranean, because I believe in its youth, because I believe in its genius, which is eternal, eternally creative" (Audisio 1936,122-23).

---

[51] "The real break," as I wrote previously (Meldolesi 2006, 80, n. 11), "occurs with the establishment of Rome."
[52] Cf. above, n. 19.
[53] Cf., above, n. 39.

IV

8 — To complete this first tour of the landscape, on the other hand, we must now discuss *La culture indigene. La nouvelle culture méditerranéenne* [The indigenous culture. The new Mediterranean culture] by Albert Camus[54] — the inaugural lecture for the "House of Culture" in Algiers (8 February 1937)[55] — still seen as a kind of "Manifesto" launching "la pensée de midi."[56]

The text is divided into six sections. The first of these argues that "The 'House of Culture' that we are inaugurating today wishes to contribute to the creation of a local area culture. It aspires to serve Mediterranean culture. This cannot, however, be a sort of 'sunshine nationalism.' The Mediterranean around us is a living corm try, while nationalism always appears in history as a symptom of decadence. When the vast edifice of the Holy Roman Empire collapsed, when the spiritual unity disintegrated that had given so many different worlds their reason for living, then and only then did nationalities appear. Since then, the West has never managed to regain its unity. At present, it is internationalism that aims to restore to the West its actual meaning and vocation. Only the principle is no longer Christian, it is no longer papal Rome. The principle is man. Unity no longer resides in religious faith, but in hope."

Thus, in this text the utopian impulse is proposed in a general

---

[54] Roger Grenier (1987, 28) states that in *Le Courage*, one of his earliest writings, Camus (as a young intellectual influenced by Paul Valery via Jean Grenier, and then, above all, philosophically and emotionally attracted to Nietzsche) had already shown some typical characteristics of his thinking: "a tragic feeling about life, the need to forge a morality, distrust of rationalism, Mediterranean mystique, revolt and acceptance, reverse and obverse." Joining the Algerian Communist Party in 1936, he was primarily involved in the theater and soon became general secretary of the new "House of Culture" — an organization that was part of the "Popular Front," which was created at the initiative of the Party's Parisian leadership.

[55] Initially published in the first issue (May 1937) of *Jeune Méditerranée*, newsletter of the House of Culture of Algiers (evidently referring in the title to the two volumes by Gabriel Audisio discussed above). In this lecture, as Roger Grenier observed (1987, 38): Albert Camus "contrasting Francis of Assisi with Luther, and to some extent the Italy that remains human despite the Duce with the Germany that marches in step with Hitler, [...] sketches out [...] the doctrine of the 'pensée de midi' that would become the conclusion of L' *Homme révolté*."

[56] This lecture, as Neil Foxlee (2010, 51) states, "has usually been discussed in the context of Camus's life and work as a whole, where it has been seen as important for two very different reasons. First, it has been seen as the earliest formulation of a 'Mediterranean humanism' central to Camus's world-view," [...] and "second, from a postcolonial viewpoint." But to my knowledge it has never been considered part of the theoretical-practical embryo of a collective point of view that still awaits true explicit expression and its own development.

way, in an anti-nationalist political key inspired by the Popular Front of France at the time. Camus is asking: is a new Mediterranean culture feasible? This is the theme of the second section, based on "objective facts."[57] When a person travels around Europe and comes back to Italy and Provence, they are relieved to find people who are not restrained and repressed — they find the vigorous, colorful life that we know.

"This is the Mediterranean, an odor, a fragrance that there is no point in describing — we can all feel it under our skin. Moreover, whenever a doctrine has encountered the Mediterranean basin, in the resulting collision of ideas it has always been the Mediterranean that has prevailed. For example, for those who have recently lived in Germany and Italy, it is an obvious fact that fascism does not wear the same face in the two countries. It is a Mediterranean miracle that allows people who think humanly to live without oppression in a country [Italy] that has inhuman laws."

The third section rails against a manifesto signed by twenty-four Western intellectuals extolling the Abyssinian War — praising Italy's civilizing mission in barbaric Ethiopia. There are echoes in Camus's text of Audisio's tirade against Rome and Latinity, even to the point that he willingly concedes Mussolini's claim to be the true successor of the ancient Caesars, as long as it is understood by this that, as in their case, he is sacrificing truth and greatness for senseless violence. We do not want the lie that has triumphed in Ethiopia, the section concludes, but the truth that is being assassinated in Spain.[58]

North Africa — and this is the theme of the fourth section — represents one of the few areas of the world where East and West live together. At this meeting point, there is no difference between the way of life of a Spaniard or an Italian from the Algerian coast and the Arabs around them. What is most essential about Mediterranean genius springs perhaps from this encounter, unique in history and geography, between East and West.[59] In so many different ways, the Mediterranean thus offers us the image of a tangible, living and diverse civilization, one that transforms doctrines in its own image — and receives ideas without changing its own nature.

Why go any further? Camus asks at this point. And his answer is that the Mediterranean must transform today's doctrines. This is the

---

[57] For brevity' sake, I inevitably exclude here many examples found in the text.
[58] A dear allusion to the war that was then going on in Spain.
[59] Here the text refers explicitly to the work of Audisio.

subject of the fifth section. At present, the battle for collectivism, he writes, is not being fought in Russia, but in the Mediterranean basin and in Spain. Before our eyes there are realities that are stronger than ourselves. Our ideas must adapt to them. We need to rehabilitate the Mediterranean. To discover what is concrete and alive in it and encourage the different aspects of its culture. An essential role for cities like Algiers and Barcelona is to minister, in their own modest way, to that aspect of Mediterranean culture that encourages people and does not destroy them.

In closing, this inaugural lecture acknowledges that the role of the intellectual in our time is difficult. For those who do not wish to dodge their responsibilities, the essential task is to rehabilitate intelligence by regenerating the material they are working on, giving back to the mind all its meaning, and bringing back to culture its true face, wholesome and sunny.

We intend to bring culture back to life. The Mediterranean that surrounds us with smiles, sun and sea teaches us a lesson about this. Everything that is alive is ours. Politics is made for people, and not people for politics. A Mediterranean politics is necessary for the Mediterranean people. Is a new Mediterranean culture compatible with our social ideal feasible? Yes. But it is up to us and to you to lend a hand in making it happen.

9 — So at this point I asked myself how all this might be related to the Mediterranean project my collaborators and I have been working on all these years?

In the first place, *The Game of the Gods* and *Carlo Cattaneo and the Italian Spirit* refer (by definition) to Italy.[60] To be compared with the work of Audisio and Camus in the 1930s, they must be seen as part of the question — the part that concerns only a section of the northern Mediterranean (and the Mezzogiorno in particular). Then this must be integrated with the other northern parts and, especially, those of the southern Mediterranean. To this end, the argument — as we will see better below — can regain its forward momentum (fortunately!) from *Sel de la mer*. Having clarified this, we can 'get down to business' and quickly establish some basic points.

The first surprise is that *(mutatis mutandis')* Jeunesse, *The Game*, and

---

[60] By way of Sabatino Moscati and a line from Pliny the Elder: "this is Italy, dear to the gods" (Meldolesi 2006,13).

Carlo Cattaneo have a similar origin. They start with a negative historical turning point — the coming Second World War in the case of Audisio's two books, and Islam-inspired terrorism in mine.

The second surprise is that the four books examine Mediterranean and Western culture *'ab ovo,'* exploring its origins and citing ancient history to illuminate our present trajectory and imagine its future. They are grounded in a need for policy — implicit in the 'Algerian' inspiration, explicit (as we shall see below) in my own.

The third surprise is that they are based on an inverse relation (and one observed at a distance in time). This is to say that the imperialist rivalries of the thirties led Audisio to take shelter in the *southern* Mediterranean, while, as we shall see later, the explosion of Islamic terrorism that characterized the beginning of the third millennium led me to seek refuge in the ancient history of the *northern* Mediterranean.

More precisely, however, both of these meditations are about the Mediterranean and were initially inspired by the local youthful experiences of Audisio, Camus, and me.[61] At the same time, because of the lives they led subsequently, the books basically originate *outside* the main places they refer to (Algiers and Tunis on the one hand, the Mezzogiorno on the other). In this way, by means of an internal-external interaction with these environments, they have dug into the problem of actually bringing out the *genius loci* - the underlying condition upon which to position the eventual solution to the observed problems.

It is a valuable, exciting activity, but one that is challenging, daunting almost. Not least because, among other things, it has to do with the great open wound — between the so- called Greco-Roman heritage and the Hebrew-Semitic[62] tradition — that cleaves the Mediterranean and, while internal to the Algerian colony according to Audisio and Camus, is mostly *external* to our Mezzogiorno, despite recent immigration. (And yet it was already present in the southern-oriented work of my collaborators and myself, as an indirect effect of the ancient legacy of the Italian semi-colony — principally Sardinian and Sicilian). As desirable as it might be, unfortunately the suture is not yet in sight. We need to figure out how to deal with it — both on the respective sides of the two shores and in their relationship with one another.

In retrospect, on the other hand, it is clear that the internationalist proposal envisioned by Camus in 1937 in the footsteps of the Workers'

---

[61] Algerian for Audisio and Camus, and Positanese and Catanese in my case.
[62] Cf. above, n. 43.

Movement of the time did not 'work.' It later inspired him to an extremely interesting restatement of "la pensée de midi" (addressed later, in Part Two of this paper), which collided, however, with the onset of the Algerian War. Our own experience, on the other hand, took us through economics, Hirschman and Colorni, and the Mezzogiorno, but in the end had to recognize its own limits and make itself available for future meetings with other actors from different Mediterranean shores.

Let us proceed in order.

As I have already mentioned, the general approach of *Sel de la mer, Jeunesse's* second book, is different from that of the first. This time the focus is on Tunisia and thus on the central Mediterranean (observed from the south) instead of the western Mediterranean. Clearly, an understanding of the western Mediterranean basin was for Audisio no longer enough for an understanding of the eastern part as well (as he had initially maintained). What was needed, rather, was an exploration of the intercommunicating, and perhaps even interactive, relationship between the two basins.

Furthermore, the central Mediterranean is explicitly observed from the south, correcting the more common inverse tendency. On either shore *Sel de la mer* represents an important step forward in the analysis of the Mediterranean 'compass rose.' All this, in turn, allows an appropriate focus on the central Mediterranean as seen from the south.

Audisio's purpose was political and cultural. With his re-evaluation of Carthage, he sought among other things to overcome current prejudice against Semites and Jews, and with his invective against Rome (diabolical, hated since childhood, etc.) he also wanted to fight against traditional Roman-Latin nationalist-imperialist thinking. On both sides, his aim was to propose a cultural re-balancing vis-a-vis the Mediterranean that would allow increased genuine appreciation of this "middle sea" and the peoples who gravitate to it.

Nevertheless, a real explanation of why (and how) things 'went the way they did' still does not emerge. At some point there is a risk of losing the thread of the argument (and with it the glimmer of truth it undoubtedly contains). One would have to defer to history. From here it becomes 'expedient' to trouble Braudel (and Cattaneo). This is what I intend to suggest in the next chapter.

10 — In conclusion, from this first reconnaissance I can see five points *a retenir* (as the French say).

- Audisio and Camus express some common beliefs about the Mediterranean. Given the difference in their ages (13 years) it seems clear to me that the former theorized these, and the latter took them up and 'adapted' them for immediate political-cultural purposes.
- Camus maintains that nationalism springs from the dissolution of empire, but later returns to Audisio's argument against Rome and Latinity. The consequence is that empire comes out of nationalism. In other words, there is a kind of 'historical spiral' of nationalism and empire that tends to replicate itself.[63]
- Camus's Mediterranean internationalist and collectivist solution, however ingenious (and perhaps paradoxical[64]), represents a kind of *deus ex machina* and is soon repudiated through his expulsion from the Algerian Communist Party.
- If we accept Colorni's criticism of proletarian internationalism,[65] reason points to a sort of federalism − in other words, Mediterranean unity corresponding to the European unity of Ventotene. Utopian as it may be at present, this proposition fits most closely with Audisio's point of view. But perhaps even this is not enough, since the true goal, however complex and long-term, is *escape* from hegemonism and the logic of domination/subordination characteristic of triumphant nationalism and imperialism − and federalism represents only *one part* of the ingenious set of tools that could be used for this alternative purpose.
- To improve our understanding, then, all that remains is to retrace our steps and plunge into the archaic era of Carthage vs. Rome as a key to the genesis of the 'historical spiral' discussed above, starting with the problem that has long respectively distressed the two reflective positions. How and why does deranged nationalism clamor for war? (Audisio and Camus's). How was 9/11 with its tragic consequences even possible? (mine).

---

[63] This is an idea which, as we shall see, can be represented with three elements instead of two: city-state, nation, empire).
[64] "The new militant [Albert Camus]," wrote Roger Grenier (1987,36), "endeavors to reconcile, paradoxically, two goals that seem very far from each other: Mediterranean culture and collectivism. But perhaps this is merely a flight of fancy...."
[65] Colorni 1944; now 2019,100-101.

CHAPTER 2

"A Plunge into the Archaic"*

There are many points of view for analyzing the Mediterranean. We saw several of these in the first chapter. Other approaches may emerge as well if new heretical actors in the "middle sea" heed the call. I hope they do.

However, while waiting for this to happen, it seems inevitable that we look to those already under discussion. I believe, in particular, that the second perspective — that of *Sel de la mer* - can be taken as a point of reference for what I would like to relate. For in fact, as I have said, a 'supplementary inquiry' is needed for it to be able to present fully its theses on Carthage and Rome.[66]

I will therefore return to the issue of colonization, from which — as mentioned above — the power of Carthage later arose. The sixth chapter of Fernand Braudel's *Memory and the Mediterranean* has a rather intriguing title in this regard, "Colonization: The Discovery of a Mediterranean 'America' in the Tenth to Sixth Centuries BC" It is clear at a glance that this cannot be about a "discovery" (in the usual sense of the word), since commercial trade in the central Mediterranean among Cypriot, Minoan, and later Mycenaean merchants already had a long history.

So what does this refer to?

---

* With some modifications, the exposition in this chapter and the following one draw largely on Chapters 1 and 2 of *Il giuoco degli dei* and Chapters 1 and 3 of *Carlo Cattaneo e lo spirito Italiano* (Soveria Marinelli, Rubbettino, 2006 and 2013a).

[66] Such an approach helps me escape from the national dimension, and at the same time covers the central Mediterranean (and therefore also concerns Italy). And finally, it invites us to look "from the bottom up" at this key area, our balancing point between East and West (and not only from top to bottom or left to right [or vice versa] as we are used to doing). In other words, it corrects (implicitly, potentially) some typical ways of thinking whose origins are often ethnocentric, Eurocentric, or nationalist, if not downright imperialist and warmongering. Uris is a need that can never be completely satisfied since as we shall see below, more 'supplementary inquiries' will be necessary (rooted in history from differing vantage points) for Audisio's claim to truly convince us so that its consequences can be resourcefully explored. More sorties will be needed outside the narrowness of the national perspective (which still tends to catch up with yours truly and still remains a key, ever-present dimension). More initiatives will need to be devised "from the bottom up" (far beyond what the following pages suggest) to redress the cognitive and normative balance regarding the central Mediterranean.

After an initial section on prehistory and the flowering of civilization in the eastern Mediterranean, Braudel's *Memory* takes up the Mediterranean world that concerns us in that it became the destination and land of choice for Phoenician and Greek colonizers. They discovered, that is, the importance of establishing their own colonies there. As mentioned, this is an "Ionian" perspective, different from those discussed up to now — in the sense that while Audisio's first *Jeunesse* book observes the Mediterranean from the West, Braudel's *Memory* considers it instead from the East. But neither of them really looks in depth at how things were on the ground *before* the colonizing movement was unleashed.

In other words, there is a problem within the problem. Just as in the case of the 'Carthage question,' a supplementary inquiry is required for Fernand Braudel's 'discovery of an America.' For this it is worth a look at the work of Carlo Cattaneo, the great intellectual patriot of the Italian Risorgimento (which Braudel probably did not consider or did not know about).

I

1 — "The European," Cattaneo wrote, "found America and Australia in the same state in which the Asian apparently found Europe. Here too, before great nations there had to be small-scale peoples, and before peoples the separate tribes. And each tribe, inhabiting a secluded valley and a heath surrounded by swamps and broken by rivers, was at first on its own as far as language and custom, confined to the narrow circle which enemy tribes marked out around it [...] [This was] long *before Eastern civilization,* [67]- penetrating with its colonies, with its priests and its merchants, with the weapons of conquest and the

---

[67] Cattaneo, 1844a; now 1957, 791-2, in "Sul principio istorico delle lingue europee" (1841b; now 1957, 446). In order to clarify this point, he had asked his readers to go back in their minds "to those times when the aboriginal hordes of Europe lay [...] divided among themselves, without self-awareness, entangled in thickets and swamps," and to imagine, "a short distance away, the great priestly empires which in Persia, Babylon, and Egypt erected superb wharves, still admirable in their ruins. How is it possible that these two ways of living, not separated from each other by deserts, as in inner Asia, did not enter into a relationship of back-and-forth reaction to one another? Tire most persecuted, the most unhappy, the most needy among the flourishing and civilized peoples had to seek the hope of a better lot, a refuge, a prize, among the savages of the north, by the route where contact was easiest and most continuous — therefore not through the Urals or the Caucasus, then walled off by marshes on account of the not yet depressed level of the Caspian, but rather through the Hellespont, and once navigation had been discovered, all along the shores of the Mediterranean."

miseries of exile and servitude, spread all along the seas and rivers of Europe, propagating *the arcane linguistic unity* which to our wonder ties us to India and Persia."[68]

"The relationship between the Asian and Europe," I have in turn argued (Meldolesi 2013a, 26, n), "is thus analogous to what was later to develop between the European and the indigenous peoples of America and Australia — but with the *crucial* difference that the former took place over a much longer time span, in successive waves by land and sea, and through trade and invasion, *long before* the Greeks and Phoenicians established their colonies in Italy and the latter became, as Braudel writes, 'an America in antiquity."[69] This explains how and why the indigenous element, instead of succumbing to the invader from the East, was able to gradually absorb its lessons, and thus build the foundations of a different — Western — civilization."

2 — The *background*, so to speak, to the whole issue was clearly of enormous importance. In all probability, a significant cultural influence on the Mediterranean from the East already existed in the third millennium; it is documented from the second millennium BC on.[70]

---

[68] "The Sanskrit language," as Cattaneo makes clear in "Dell'India" (1845; now 1942, 30), "is related in conformation and roots to the languages of Persia — indeed of all Europe — and its influence is most manifest in the favellas of those parts of the Indian peninsula which are nearest to Persia [present-day Pakistan], while they fade away toward the south. Likewise, the writing of that ancient language proceeds by vowels and consonants, like Greek and Latin, rather than by consonants alone, like the Arabic languages, or by syllables, like the Chinese, much less by hieroglyphs, like Egyptian — and it shows in this the signs of a less remote origin." Domenico Patassini — and I am grateful to him — informed me that this traditional linguistic thesis has been challenged by Giovanni Semeraro (2005) in favor, instead, of an indigenous, Aegean, Mediterranean genesis of our language. I ask the reader to take this into account in the quotes that follow from Cattaneo and Pallottino.

[69] Braudel 1998, 223 and ff.; Meldolesi 2006, Chap. 1

[70] One of the most exciting artifacts of this influence is the oxhide-shaped copper ingot (or stretcher-shaped, because it has four handles that make it easy to carry). Already in use in Cyprus in the mid-third millennium BC, it was used in exchanges with Sardinia in the mid-second millennium. In fact, sixteen such ingots have been found on the island. (I am certainly not claiming, with this small example, to penetrate the complex processes that emerge from the mists of time and challenge our understanding. Consider the majestic appearance — in the fifth-fourth millennium BC — of thirty megalithic temples in Malta; and of similar temples in Calabria and Apulia. Consider the emergence in very early prehistoric times of an indigenous ceramic production in many different localities — a highly differentiated production that passed through successive stages of development. And again, consider the flourishing of specific, localized civilizations during the Bronze Age — third to second millennium BC: the Villanovan civilization that came from the north and produced settlements with dwellings on piles, the Sardinian civilization that produced the extraordinary proliferation of three thousand *nuraghi*; the inland settlements and early writings; and those in more restricted areas

Cattaneo had long been concerned with the linguistic influence of the East on the West. He had written (Cattaneo 1841b; now 1957, 448), for example, that "according to this principle [historical, concerning European languages], Europe therefore appeared as enclosed by a great bow whose string is the Mediterranean, along which the primitive navigators propagated the civic motor of the two lineages, Semitic and IndoPersian. The Phoenicians, the Egyptians and perhaps the Etruscans were connected to the former; the Pelasgians, the Phrygians, the Venetians, the Latins and perhaps the Tuschi [...] to the latter. And perhaps other lesser *primordial civilizations* had already begun in Europe and Asia, which were overwhelmed and enveloped by them, like scattered ponds joined by a vast flood."[71]

"Great was the influence that both the Indo-Persian and Semitic nations exerted on Europe," Cattaneo went on to state, "with their colonies, merchants, artisans, warriors, priests, refugees, and captives unceasingly scattered even to the most remote interior regions. The Phoenician ships landed in Lusitania and Ireland; the oldest records speak of Egyptians, Lydians, Phrygians, and above all Pelasgians and Phoenicians, everywhere flushing out, as it were, the native barbarism" (1841b, now 1957, 417).

3 — Obviously, these far-reaching external influences had long been conversant with the internal affairs of the indigenous peoples.

"As a consequence," wrote Cattaneo (1841b, now 1957, 417), "civilization emerged for us three thousand years ago,[72] amidst the commerce of the Ligurians, the Umbrians, the Veneti, the Pelagos, and the

---

that followed trajectories of their own that we know little about or cannot yet decode. But in all likelihood, it was with the intensification of contact with the East during the second millennium BC that the fundamentally repetitive and settled life of the bulk of the population began to change, through gradual insertion into the world economy of the time. It was a trend toward incorporation that was likely to produce an acceleration of the civilizing process and was a prelude to a significant rise of the central Mediterranean).

[71] "This *metaphor* of ponds and flooding," as I commented previously (Meldolesi 2013a, 113), "seems particularly felicitous to me, because it offers at once an idea of the variety and uniformity, the multiplicity and complexity of the civilizing process". In this regard, moreover, there is a map published by Massimo Pallottino (1984, 65): "at the end of the pre-Roman era, Italy was still divided between 'non-Indo-European (or not ascertainably Indo-European) languages' such as Etruscan, Ligurian, Rhaetic, Celtic, Elimo, and Phoenician, on the one hand; and 'Indo-European languages' such as Western Italic (of which Latin appears to be one), Venetie, Eastern Italic (Osco-Umbrian), Messapic, and Greek. As can be seen, it was *only later*, with the advent of Rome, that Semitic influence was finally rejected, and Latin emerged as the prevailing language." (Meldolesi 2013a, 117).

[72] At the end of the second millennium BC, well before the Phoenician and Greek colonizations.

Etruscans. The art of masonry, unknown then beyond the Alps, painting and modeling, the custom of cohabiting in cities with polite manners, elegant pomp, and ingenious spectacles, of commemorating the events of public and private life with monuments, of adorning in religious garb measures intended for the progress of the people — these would in a few generations elevate our country almost to a modern level of culture. And Tyrrhenian navigation would unite it with all civilized peoples. The cultivation of wheat was widespread among us with the cult of Saturn, the hills were adorned with vines, and commerce was already bringing these sweet fruits of civilization to the barbarians beyond the mountains."

Among the main protagonists of this exploit, Cattaneo cited mountain people *("the hard people born from the oaks"* [Cattaneo 1841b, now 1957, 436][73] creators of Apennine culture) and the Etruscans. "From whatever point it had moved," he wrote [about the Etruscan League of the twelve republics of Tuscany], "this Hanseatic League of the ancient epoch held all the points of Italy and the islands, and encompassed all with its commerce, with its rites, with its aboriginal tribal law, in times before the Italo-Greek era. Indeed, they seem to have undertaken great works at the mouths of the Po and built its first embankments" (Cattaneo, 1844a; now 1957, 799).[74]

It was thought that the predominant influence of this civilizing process had moved from north to south. But this was not the case, wrote Massimo Pallottino, based on the "the massive and accelerated progress of archaeological, linguistic and historical knowledge in the last decades" of the last century.

---

[73] All the writers, Cattaneo went on to write (1844a, now 1957,793), "while speaking of colonies that landed in Italy from the East, and of adventurous tribes that descended little by little from the Alps, always say that Italy had even older inhabitants. And to specify that they spoke languages of their own [...] they called them aborigines [...]; they called them mountain dwellers, frugal, strong agrarians, hard at arms, hard as the oaks of their native forests [...]. *Nor were those lineages ever extinguished, nor driven elsewhere;* and several times they reestablished *the population of the open country,* exterminated by sudden calamities. And yet we see them descend every year to assist [people] in the labors of the fields, and keep them numerous in their city arts; foundation and nerve of the nation; eternal rejuvenating source of that variety of character and wit, which we admire in the individual peoples of Italy, and which some vainly deplore. *This progeny was the raw material,* on which eastern influence imprinted only its form."

[74] At some point, then, before the Italo-Greek era, Etruscan federalism (in arms, trade, rites and law) became dominant in Italy — able to undertake even major public works. Moreover, Cattaneo's retrospective cultural reference to the Renaissance Hanseatic League of Northern Europe evidently suggests (in reverse) that, on our continent, a small federalist tradition had indeed already been inaugurated by the Etruscans...

"The old image of a primitive Italy populated and civilized by incursions from the north has been *turned upside down* by discoveries showing the existence of developed, sophisticated and enduring neolithic cultures in the Italian Mezzogiorno and the islands, of Bronze Age civilizations of the type dubbed 'Apenninic' spread across the entire peninsula [...], of marked and repeated influences from the eastern Mediterranean Orient, which culminated in the presence of Mycenaean traders, who may even have been in some sense colonists, in Apulia and the Sicilian region, as well as along the Tyrrhenian coast and in Sardinia; and of the practice of cremation in southern Italy at a date no later than it is found in the north, demonstrating the importance and antiquity of local advances in the peninsula and islands and the important function of Mediterranean contacts and influences" (Pallottino 1984, 40 e 40-1; emphasis added).

II

4 — Let us look at colonization.[75] Fernand Braudel[76] has maintained that the first to arrive in the central and western Mediterranean were "probably the Phoenicians"[77] But today it is thought that they arrived around the same time as the settlers from Greece.[78] "There is no

---

[75] Clearly, the argument about the possible formation of a "colonial style" cannot be limited to Greek influence, which would be an error of content and method. As often happens, it would be a first step in precisely the sort of simplifying reductionism that we are aiming here to refute. Much of our current scholastic historiography leans toward a Rome-centric (and nationalist, Occidentalist, etc.) approach, which tends to summarize (or subsume) everything within the republican and imperial history of Rome. Thus, it happens that the Phoenicians are mentioned in passing, the Greeks are turned into the "cultural artifact" of ancient Greece, Italic peoples pre-exist Rome only to be assimilated by it later, and Carthage is the "*delenda*" par excellence, etc. Instead, by overturning the unreasonable 'dumbing down' produced by such historiography, it is possible to rediscover the great richness of the multiplicities and interrelationships of 'so much history.'
[76] Braudel 1998, passim (sec. 4-8): 223-48.
[77] "The people whom the Greeks called *Phoenikes*," Braudel writes, "the Red People (no doubt because of their famous purple cloth), and whom we call Phoenicians, were directly descended from the Semitic Canaanites, who had long been settled on the Syrian-Palestinian coast." "Their woolen fabrics are famous, as are the dyes-extracted from a mollusk, the *murex*. This essential industry was set up far from the cities, however, because it was necessary to leave the flesh of the mollusks to decompose for a long period in the open air, in a soaking area that gave off an abominable odor. Huge quantities of *murex* shells point to numerous dyeing workshops, both in Phoenician territory and in the western colonies."
[78] The specific causes of such migratory waves would need a study of their own. To get an idea, I would point out that the initial 'draw' for Phoenician colonization was probably growth — and primarily the search for metals as a critical means of dominating the high-end trade aimed

mystery about the Phoenicians or the Greeks. The former came from the coastal regions of the Levant, the latter from the Aegean [...]; both had behind them an advanced civilization, [...] the intense activity of the cities, techniques of navigation and metalworking, the practice of trading and the power of the markets."[79]

"The ancient Phoenicia of the Levant," Braudel added, "consisted of a strip of land whose width varied from twelve kilometers to barely fifty [...]. It was a chain of small ports, short valleys, hills, eroded slopes, and insignificant coastal islands. By land, cities communicated poorly, but fortunately they could do so by sea. Each of these ports thought of itself as an independent universe. Because they had chosen to settle on easily defended capes or islands, they turned their backs on the mountainous hinterland."

Tyre, for example, which would have a very prominent role in the Phoenician colonization of the Mediterranean, "was built on a narrow island where the town found its essential: a defense [...], two harbors, a natural one to the north [...] an artificial one to the south [...] and finally, located in the sea itself, a bubbling spring of fresh drinking water [...]. Thereafter, the Phoenicians constantly strove to recreate this ideal urban geography in their colonial settlements, situating them where possible on islands or promontories."

5 — Industrious by necessity, the Phoenician cities of the Levant "all had an active class of artisans: weavers, metalworkers, jewelers, shipbuilders. [...] Phoenician 'industries' excelled in everything. Their woolen fabrics were as famous as their dyes [...] whose shades ranged

---

primarily at the rising Mediterranean aristocracies. At a later stage, however, the military defeat of the homeland by the Assyrians along with the Babylonian occupation of Tyre likely played a key role in the 'push' toward Carthage. As for the Greeks, in addition to the search for metals, their much larger and more dispersed numbers suggest ease of access to the southern Italian coasts, overpopulation relative to the resources available in their places of origin, and the greater iron content of the soils to be colonized — without excluding, at a later stage, the indirect effect produced by the pressure on the motherland of the Persian empire.

[79] It should not be imagined, however, that the two peoples were motivated by mutually 'amorous feelings.' "According to the author of the Odyssey," Warmington (1968, 36-7) writes, "the Phoenicians had a very bad reputation [...]. On the face of it, this hostile (we were about to say 'anti-Semitic') attitude goes back to a period of rivalry or competition between the Greeks and the Phoenicians in the West, which can be dated [...] after the beginning of the eighth century [...], nor is it to be assumed that Greek merchants were more respectable at that time. In any case, a prejudice of class as well as of race was involved. The aristocratic audience of the poems would identify themselves with the Greek heroes, for whom it was laudable to get wealth by piratical raids but not by trade; when the Phoenicians did rob they did it ingloriously, by stealth; and one of the most humiliating insults was to be taken for a merchant."

from pink to purple to violet." Not to mention ivory plates, silver or gold cups, glass (beads, amulets, pendants, perfume vials, small polychrome vases), ceramics, etc. This manufacturing gave rise to intense commercial activity, including the brokering of others' goods as well.

Accomplished sailors, the Phoenicians plied the seas in boats with meticulously tarred hulls. They followed three Mediterranean routes: northern, southern, and the central "island" route. They created bases on headlands and islets where if needed they could later develop colonies.[80] Carthage was initially just one of their many destinations, but it is located in a strategic position.[81]

According to the latest reconstructions,[82] the Phoenician colonial phenomenon is quite complex. As mentioned, it gained impetus by resuming a long association with the central and western Mediterranean,[83] and was initially a product of an expansion, not a crisis, of the community of origin.[84]

Its predominant commercial characteristic is rooted in the extraction of metal ores and the existence of high- ranking partners (and local buyers). In other words, it formed part of the aristocratic trade

---

[80] The founding of Phoenician colonies, as Warmington clarified (ibid., 39), "is a consequence of the need for safe anchorages and water supply bases on the long route to Spain. [...] Given the general practice of anchoring each night, the locations known to Phoenician sailors must have been far more numerous than those that later became permanent colonies, and the growth of the latter must have been determined by the nature of the hinterland and the need to defend key points along the routes."

[81] Qart Hadasht or the 'new city' in Phoenician. "Situated at the meeting place of the western and eastern Mediterranean," Braudel wrote, "it was easy for Carthage to take advantage of the immense difference in their economic and cultural levels. The west was barbarian and underdeveloped. Carthage could obtain everything cheaply there, including metals: tin from the Cassiterides [islands to the north, beyond the strait of Gibraltar] and north-western Spain; lead, copper and above all silver from Andalusia and Sardinia; gold dust from sub-Saharan Africa [...]; and, finally, slaves, wherever they could be captured, at times even on the high seas."

[82] Cf. Bondì 2003.

[83] "The Phoenicians introduced new technologies in Sicily, where at the turn of the second and early first millennia the first iron artifacts are attributed to them, and in Spain where their contribution is marked by new techniques for exploiting mineral resources." (Ibid., 66-7).

[84] Cf. above, n. 78. "The initiation of colonial expansion is one of the most vital expressions of a society which, at the beginning of the first millennium BC, at the height of its political and economic prosperity, exercised a veritable 'magisterium of culture' in the Syro-Palestinian area." (Ibid., 68). The economy and the cultural and political life of Phoenician cities were initially organized around the palace. (In particular, the city of Biblos initiated the creation of the alphabet, which became established among neighboring populations and later inspired the Greek alphabet.) But subsequently, Phoenician cultural and economic prosperity supported the establishment of a class of private shipowners and merchants. These were the real protagonists of colonial expansion.

which, after the great crisis of the "peoples of the sea,"[85] was again asserting itself in the Mediterranean.

Taking advantage of the "island route" and the southern route (against the wind on the way out and to windward on the way back) and aiming first and foremost at the Iberian Peninsula, rich in metal resources, the Phoenicians, over a century and a half (between the first half of the 8th and the second half of the 7th centuries) and in successive waves, created dozens of colonial bases — sometimes on a headland overlooking the sea, sometimes on a small island close to the mainland, or even in a broad gulf.

These colonies were diversified: for protection of the sea lanes, as trade bases, for metal supply, and as settlements. Soon, they began to run their own very successful trade circuits (including, of course, those with the local populations).

6 — On this subject, Sabatino Moscati's book, *La bottega del mercante. Artigianato e commercio fenicio lungo le sponde del Mediterraneo* (1996) [The Merchant's Workshop. Phoenician Craft and Trade along the Shores of the Mediterranean] is particularly insightful, arguing that Phoenician crafts and trade played a basic role in inter-Mediterranean exchange down through the ages.[86]

The book surveys places of craft production: in the Near East (the figured terracottas, sarcophagi, ivories,[87] cups); in Africa (archaic stelae, terracottas, protomes and masks, razors); in Spain (jewelry, ivories,

---

[85] I am referring, clearly, to the striking series of catastrophic events that occurred between the end of the Bronze Age and the Iron Age. "By the time the waters subsided, the Hittite empire was destroyed, the Babylonian empire of the Gassites was close to collapse, Egypt was heading for a period of decline, the Mycenaean kingdoms were no more than a memory, and the Po Valley, in which 'Terramare' settlements had sprung up during the Bronze Age with a density, in certain areas, of one every 5 kilometers, was almost deserted" (Manfredi 2004,11).

[86] It is a text that stresses the very long term, so much so that it dedicates the volume "to the merchants of the souks, unchanging through time." "In today's souks," the author (1996, x) explains, "a reality almost three thousand years old is repeated and renewed (...), one that has defied time and presents itself in terms of living interests, posing questions that strike both the curious visitor and the committed historian. Where did the products come from, what was their nature, what was the mechanism of their distribution? How did the artisans work, commissioned by whom (...)? What was their relationship with the merchants (...)? In the answer (or rather in the answers) to these questions lies the secret of a great civilization that defied time, that formed the foundations of our own civilization on opposite Mediterranean shores." This is a piece in the puzzle that we must not let slip through our fingers!

[87] The cover shows an extraordinary "Panel with a lion mauling a black man, in ivory, gold and precious stones," a product of Phoenician craftsmanship, then probably a spoil of war, found at Nimrud, an Assyrian city in northern Iraq.

decorated ostrich eggs); and in Italy (stelae, jewelry).

"The primacy of Tharros (on the western Sardinian coast)," Moscati wrote, "is clearly linked to the city's status as a great international emporium, according to the evidence the largest in the western Mediterranean, the point of convergence for components of a commercial traffic that radiated from it in every direction. The more we learn about it, the more Tharros appears to us as a grand souk or bazaar, dealing in goods (...) that came from everywhere, so that it is likely that even the local workshops were for the most part unable to distinguish their origin" (124).

Unfortunately, until a short while ago little was known about the Phoenician world and its extraordinary influence on ancient Italy, above all western Sicily and Sardinia. In recent decades, knowledge has significantly increased, even to the point that a small network of local museums related to Phoenician settlements has been set up in Sardinia.[88]

Tharros (in the Oristano area) at one point became the main Phoenician emporium in the Mediterranean — not least because it was on the route to the Balearic Islands and Spain, where the Phoenicians ventured in search of metals. Phoenician, Sardinian, and Spanish silver mines undoubtedly played a significant role in the Phoenician colonial network, especially for high-end Mediterranean trade.

The Phoenician colonial bases enjoyed broad autonomy. With time, some of them tended to evolve into city-states. When the homeland was gradually subjugated by the Assyrian and then Babylonian empires in the 7th and 6th centuries BC, a new wave of Phoenician colonization took place in the central and western Mediterranean. In effect independent by that time, Carthage emerged in this galaxy as the principal city-state.[89]

---

[88] A journey around the Phoenician settlements in Sardinia has the feel of a crucial and revealing plunge into the archaic. It is this process of art-historical rediscovery that, among other things, made it possible to mount the major exhibition on the Phoenicians at Palazzo Grassi in Venice (1988).

[89] "The Carthaginians insistence on maintaining control of the route to Spain," wrote Warmington (1968, 62-3), "may be compared with the interest of the Athenians in the fifth and fourth centuries in the route to the Black Sea, from which they obtained supplies of corn for their large urban population. The exploitation of the metal production of Spain was as integral a part of Carthaginian existence as if the mines had been located a few miles from the city itself."

7 — A first-rate craft and commercial center, Carthage routinely used barter[90] (and later currency as well) in economic activities involving transportation and brokering, focusing on the extraordinary comings and goings of its shipping, and on easing the routine of its mercantile life. At the same time, it increased its presence in the hinterland, developing its agricultural productivity, gradually suppressing the Phoenician colonial system, and reorganizing it overall to its own advantage and strengthening itself militarily[91] on both land and sea.[92] This was the origin of the power of the Punic people[93] — as overseas Phoenicians were known thereafter.

"The center of Phoenician life," Braudel explains, "now shifted to Carthage, which was better situated than Tyre, at the exact meeting point of the two Mediterraneans and out of reach of foreign aggression. Phoenician civilization continued there, at once the same and different [...]. The differences were accentuated by distance, by the inevitable gap between two sets of cultural practices, and not least by the mixed origins of the town."

---

[90] A 'ritual' in dealings with indigenous peoples that inspired an astonishing page from Herodotus (ibid., 83).
[91] Including by reforming the army in the 6th century. "Up to this date, [...] the army had consisted of a citizen levy like that in any other ancient city state; from the time of Mago [a capable general who came from the most prominent family in Carthage, the army] consisted of contingents drawn from the subject states and of mercenaries, though the generals were Carthaginian. The reason for the reform was that the population of Carthage was too small to provide for the defense of so widely scattered an empire." Moreover, "it was cheaper to use the revenues of the state to hire mercenaries than to withdraw a large number of citizens from the trading activities which provided so great a part of its wealth." (Ibid. 51).
[92] This is a process that asserted itself even more in the face of adverse circumstances, especially after the defeats of the Carthaginians and their Etruscan allies in the second half of the 5th century. "This was the beginning of a dramatic period for the Carthaginians," Braudel states, "a crisis that was at once political, religious and economic. Tanit, the tutelary goddess of the city [...], became the chief deity. Carthage reacted vigorously to its economic difficulties: imports were reduced, an austerity program was put in place, and relations with sub-Saharan Africa and the Cassiterides were strengthened. Above all, Carthage fell back on North Africa, taking over a vast surrounding area for livestock-raising and orchards. [...] The long century when Carthage was on the defensive allowed the city to gain new strength and take advantage of the weakness of Athens following the failure of the Athenian expedition against Syracuse (415-409). Immediately, Carthage began to wage war ferociously against the Sicilian Greeks, attacking their towns, capturing the inhabitants and thus acquiring a slave labor force which was to transform the economy itself" [of the ascendant power].
[93] "Carthage," Braudel writes, "was able to defend its essential assets, and in particular its 'monopoly' on mining in Spain: it succeeded in keeping the Etruscans, the Greeks and then the Romans away from most of the profitable part of the Iberian Peninsula. It managed also to defend its most important maritime ports of call, its luxury industries (woven fabrics [...], ivories and furniture) and its day-to-day trading activities, notably the wholesale grain trade and the thriving salt fish industry."

"Carthage, a genuine fragment of the Orient, was not contaminated by Indo-European influences." It is the queen city that emerges from "the discovery of an America" in antiquity. It was a "materialistic, down-to-earth, fast-moving civilization, preferring the sturdy to the refined. This was a powerful city, attracting sailors, craftsmen, and mercenaries from far afield. Accepting many different cultures, it was by nature cosmopolitan. For seven centuries, it made its hard-felt mark on Mediterranean Africa, but at the same time it probably absorbed into its veins all kinds of African blood."[94]

III

8 — In light of all this, the key point (which would round out Audisio's research) ought, in my opinion, to be the analysis of the process of *transformation* (to which we will return several times, for verification) that affected the city-states in the central Mediterranean. The growing *power politics*, that is, of the poleis, and the heated rivalries that divided them and would eventually lead them to the tragic Punic Wars.

It is a process which, to be brought into focus, requires a broader expository horizon than that of *Sel de la. mer*. Indeed, at one point, by defeating Athens and asserting itself to the detriment of the Etruscans and Carthaginians, Syracuse seemed in a position to emerge as a dominant power. But its attempt was short-lived and Carthage, as I have just mentioned, was the next to try.

Finally, there was Rome, which had sprung from the partial fusion of certain Italic peoples (Etruscans, Latins, and Sabines).[95] After passing through a long and fairly drab formative period, its rapid military advance[96] gradually absorbed pre-existing human aggregations (native

---

[94] "North Africa, which had barely emerged from the Stone Age when the Phoenicians arrived, received almost everything from its new masters: fruit-trees (the olive, vine, fig, almond and pomegranate, all of whose fruits were exported to Italy), techniques of agriculture and winemaking and many craft processes. Carthage was its tutor, and the lessons went in deep."
[95] "In the early days of Rome's career, nothing seemed to single out for greatness a town which long lay dormant. There was nothing to distinguish it from the other towns in Latium." This had to wait until 338 BC, the year in which, battered by Rome, the Latin confederation collapsed. "The Latin cities were subjugated and Rome, now unfettered, was to become ruler of Italy within seventy years" through wars of attrition waged against Etruria and the south. "Forged in the course of the Latin wars, the Roman legion was the instrument of victory."
[96] Which of course was marked by ups and downs. One only has to think of the Samnite wars that left a trace even in the language through the humiliation imposed on Roman legionaries by the famous "Caudine Forks." Some historians also believe that if the meteoric Alexander the Great, instead of aiming eastward, had pushed his conquests to the west, he would most

and imported) and mercilessly destroyed those that opposed it.[97] When this process reached Sicily, confrontation with Carthage came to a head.

Thus, the wound between the Greco-Roman and Jewish-Semitic traditions within the Mediterranean was disproportionately aggravated and, even later, was never truly healed and 'sutured.' This is a recurring theme of the present work.

Attention should first of all be focused on the major issue of the domination / subordination relationship, whose trail disappears in the mists of time. This is a problem that has a long evolutionary history in the East, while tending to intensify in the West with the building of the city-states of the Phoenician and Greek settlers "armed one against the other." Thereafter, as just mentioned, the growth in economic and military power of some of them tended to consolidate their dominance on a more substantial scale of power — as compared with smaller city-states, small aggregations, territories, etc. A temporary condition of unstable imbalances between rival powers (and alliances) was thus created, whose resolution would eventually pave the way for developments that were nationalist, and then imperialist, but with an indigenous (rather than imported) heart.

"The point is, in other words, that such a history has a very different outcome from that of 'modern America' which, as is well known, was founded on the genocide of the indigenous peoples, relegating those (few) who survived to the margins. Indeed, even in this regard, the role of the *native* element in the Italian equation — Cattaneo's *'hard people born of the oaks'* — is undoubtedly crucial," both in limiting and absorbing (in part) the Phoenician and Greek thrust, and finally in allowing a different perspective.[98]

"And since this concerns not only the construction of Italy, but also the very foundations of the West, I think it must be recognized *apertis verbis* that the dawn of this great historical process includes a rainbow of different contributors: Etruscans, Italic peoples from different groups and localities, Greeks, Phoenicians, Romans. In this

---

likely have subdued Rome.

[97] It can be said that it perfected "in miniature" the scorched earth technique that it later used on a large scale against Carthage. For example, Tarquinia, an important Etruscan city-state, was burned to the ground — so that in the Middle Ages it was rebuilt on another hill by the name of Corneto. Hie contemporary behavior of the Russian Army in Chechnya, Syria and now in Ukraine indeed seems to follow the same track.

[98] While on the other hand, as it is well known, the intensive use of slavery is undoubtedly common to the two experiences.

respect, the *indigenous, original* contribution proved to be decisive" (Meldolesi 2013a, 124) — for better, or worse (it must be added).

9 - Contrary to what Audisio thought, this process is in my opinion important in helping us understand the establishment and limitations of Mediterranean civilizations. As previously announced, I include below a few pages from a text of mine from 2006, *Il giuoco degli dèi*.

"My interest in pre-Roman history — an unlikely avenue for the economic policy of the present," I wrote in the preface to that slim volume, "arose in the spring of 2001 when, in order to promote the formation of regional and provincial Commissions for non-regular labor, I began to bring together weekly [in the Capital], at the Prime Minister's Office, a group of young experts, mostly from the South. In that lively climate of discussions concerning the institutional and productive evolution of the areas with the most submerged [labor], I came up with the rather whimsical idea of collaterally pursuing, purely for pleasure, a brief exploration of the *in situ* genesis of our civilization."[99]

It was a fortunate intuition because the young people turned out to be very receptive to an archaic history that (surprisingly) had to do with... their own homes — in the sense that each young person could actually form a tie to the original people of his or her home area.[100] In addition, their reaction opened my eyes to a *preexisting* Mediterranean cultural foundation[101] to the so-called Greco-Roman heritage on

---

[99] Meldolesi 2006, 6. Evidently, once again, intuition had overpowered reason.
[100] An Italy, that is, "built at the dawn of history by the Ligurians, the Raeti, the Camuni, the Venetians, the Piceni, the Umbrians, the Latins, the Sannites, the Campanians, the Apulians, the Lucanians, the Bruttians (or Brettii), the Sicels, the Sards, the Corsicans, and of course the Etruscans." "And also by the Intimilii, the Ingauni, the Taurini, the Salassi, the Lepontii, the Celts, the Insubres, the Carni, the Histri, the Iapydes, the Illyrians, the Liburnians, the Tigullii, the Apuani, the Praetutii, the Frentani, the Vestini, the Marrucini, the Paeligni, the Caraceni, the Falisci, the Sabines, the Aequi, the Pentri, the Marsi, the Hernici, the Volsci, the Aurunci, the Sidicini, the Caudini, the Hirpini, the Daunians, the Peucetians, the Messapians, the Calabrians, the Oenotrians, the Osci, the Morgetes, the Itali, the Sicani, and the Elymians." (Ibid. 15 and n.).
[101] This is clearly not the "eternal Mediterranean" that Audisio was talking about (cf. above, sec. 1 of Chap. 1), but a 'deep' Mediterranean, earlier than the one usually spoken about. It is a Mediterranean that developed in a complex way, inevitably linked to the dominating forces that followed, but one that can be rediscovered — not least because in many of its details (perhaps only partially represented, as examples) it actually reaches down to us. Uris explains the attitude I have gradually developed with respect to Audisio's oft-repeated, categorical statements (for example, in praise of the 'eternal Mediterranean'). On the one hand I realize (obviously) that these are historically inexact theses, but on the other I can see that they contain a grain of truth that ought to be saved, especially for those who think as I do, on the basis of experience, that the cultural repository of the 'deep Mediterranean' has extraordinary

which, as claimed in schoolbooks, Western civilization is (*tout court*) supposed to rest.

In fact, as I wrote, "if one pays attention, one can almost perceive the minute footfalls of these peoples on the move. One has to be passionate about the examination of the archaic finds — from the Camuni engravings, to the terracotta statues of Lavinio, to the Lucanian funerary paintings of Paestum, to the Sardinian bronzes — to understand the extraordinary collective effort that exists at the base, both *motu proprio* and as a reaction to outside influences (Celtic or Gallic from the north, Phoenician and Greek from the south). One needs to have a grasp of the specific characteristics of the beginnings of our civilization, concerning settlements and roads,[102] topographic placement,[103] art, languages, religions, currencies, etc. — to try to understand deeds and misdeeds, processes, and trends" (Meldolesi 2006, 15).[104]

It was an extraordinary collective 'find' that today in retrospect makes me feel close to the ideas on the long Mediterranean life span of "la pensée de midi."

10 — "In this way, mindful of [Braudel's] *Memory and the Mediterranean*, which had greatly impressed me, I began to investigate the transitional era between the proto-history and history of the Peninsula, an era in which the Italic peoples left permanent traces on the very identity of our regions. Mine were small soundings, attempts at a journey to the source — hypotheses of an unlikely work which nevertheless proved very useful to me after September 11, 2001, when, in those months of torment, I tried to use some aspect of my fledgling exploration for an

---

potential, 'a lid on the cauldron of the future,' that needs to be carefully lifted.

[102] "Perhaps the most obvious example is the 'amber road,' which runs from the Baltic shores across Europe to the Veneto and Marche, winding along the Adriatic coast. This route can be said to be the centerpiece of the rediscovered Picenian civilization, with its highly prized products, some rough cores of which have been found in Belmonte, proving the role of local workshops" (Moscati 1995, 92).

[103] "A characteristic dimension of ancient Italy is its mountain civilization — the imposing centers discovered in the uplands of Molise, evidently built by the ancient Samnites, and the prehistoric figures engraved by the thousands on the rocks of Valcamonica, the largest complex in all of Europe, and a sign of an advanced civilization that lasted from about ten thousand years before Christ to the beginning of our own era." (Ivi).

[104] Ethnographic interest in the rich cultural heritage that comes to us from the Italic peoples continues to attract attention. Cf. for example, Erla Zwingle's (2005) reporting on certain aspects of contemporary folk festivals from ancient Italic peoples - such as the pyre of vine branches at the feast of S. Antonio Abate in Novoli (related to the Apuli, Apulia), the snakes at the feast of S. Domenico Abate of Cocullo (related to the Marsi, Abruzzo), and the candles of the eponymous race at the feast of S. Ubaldo in Gubbio (related to the Umbri, and to Umbria).

implicit dialogue with the reasoning that was then being framed" by the then President of the Italian Republic, Carlo Azeglio Ciampi.[105]

IV

11 — "To help you understand (and understand me) I should point out that I have long practiced the ahistorical discipline par excellence — economics. And yet, at a certain point in my research my professor of history was Fernand Braudel.[106] It happened that twenty years later, in the distress unleashed by 9/11, I instinctively found shelter in history — indeed, in archaic history. It was almost as if it were an 'air raid shelter/ like the one in World War II that I used to scramble into as a very young child, at the first wail of the sirens."[107]

Was it some vital impulse that — disrupting one of my many soliloquies — suddenly 'kidnapped' me, through a force perhaps similar to the one that had suddenly spurred Audisio to seek his own explicit 'escape route' in defending Carthage against Rome, *apertis verbis*?

Did we not feel a need, Audisio and I, to grasp, in ancient history, a key that would enable us to take an explicit stand against the indiscriminate use of violence, against "the worship of force and success through force" (Audisio 1936, 104), which has unfortunately prevailed in the nationalist and imperialist reasoning that has dominated our part of the world for the past two millennia?

Have we not been trying to 'take stock,' to learn something new from the "discovery of a Mediterranean 'America' in the tenth to sixth centuries BC" sketched by Braudel, and its extraordinary consequences?

---

[105] Without whose revealing insight, competent and patriotic in difficult times — it is worth pointing out — this line of thinking would not even have seen light of day. Because, as I mentioned in *The Game of the Gods*, "it is an unexpected child of '9/11' — that is, of the tragedy of September 11, 2001, and its dramatic wake of blood and pain" (Meldolesi 2006, 5).

[106] "There was a misunderstanding at the start. At one point, as I was pondering what to do after managing to gain some distance from the authoritarian cogency of economics, I happened upon Fernand Braudel's *Dynamics of Capitalism* (1981). I enjoyed turning its reasoning into an economic model (later published: Meldolesi 1984). So, I went to Paris to find the great historian and show it to him. Only then did I realize that he would have liked anything except for his work of so many years to be turned into a model (or rather, as I told him, into one of several possible models). But this 'pope of historians' took a liking to me: he wanted to offer me "une bouteuille de Bourgogne," he introduced me to some historians from the *Annales*, and he tried to convince me (unsuccessfully) of his methodological views on economics. In brief, he quickly taught me new ways to love history". (Ibid., n. 1).

[107] Ibid., p 5-6.

I think we have. In fact, I have glimpsed a certain parallelism between Audisio's work and mine in some initial insights related to their respective 'peregrinations' (Mediterranean, Southern). At some point, nudged by events, these unexpectedly came together, "a final straw" in explicit opposition to the conventional wisdom of the time.

We set out respectively, Gabriel and I, to look for an alternative, utopian as it may be — a "Mediterranean homeland" for Audisio, and my own yet-to-be-constructed Colornian federalization (Southern, Italian, European, Mediterranean, etc.). Yet capable, in the final analysis, of 'mirroring' (far more by difference, clearly, than by correspondence) the distant past — in the federal experiences of the Etruscan, Latin, Italic, Phoenician, and Greek city-states that had blossomed historically (mainly) in the central Mediterranean before the tragic clash between Carthage and Rome.

12   — But what could I devise on an intellectual level at a juncture as tragic as '9/11'?

"As an introduction," I had written, "I merely mention that my gravitation towards America [...] and studying the great political scientist Louis Hartz have taught me a great deal about the American people's congenital difficulty in understanding others. Thus, '9/11' immediately suggested two things to me — one was Western co-responsibility under conditions of emergency (and explicit solidarity with the hard-hit American people), and the other was concern for the future, not least because the 'red flag in front of the raging bull' effect might trigger a dangerous spiral," which then (unfortunately) actually occurred in Afghanistan, Iraq, Syria (Meldolesi 2006, 7).[108]

"It was at this point that I suddenly remembered a lesson from Fernand Braudel, according to which all of human history must be called to account to explain the present. Except that, as I was a professor of political economy as well as occupied at Palazzo Chigi, I read this suggestion backwards. Indeed, while Braudel concluded (inevitably) that one must engage with history, I expected (and still do) to find clues in the past that would help me better understand the current problems I was struggling with. This is not just a professional detour — it is also an exciting intellectual adventure.

Historians study the past with the concerns of the present world

---

[108] And went on until the precipitous abandonment of Afghanistan twenty years later — a bitter betrayal of its people, especially its women...

in mind, and these concerns change over time. For this reason, historians' studies also change over time. And this is also why, I would add, such studies can be applied in a direction contrary to how they were conceived — in other words, from the past to the present.

Therefore, to approach the crisis unleashed by '9/11' on a cultural level, I followed (at first unwittingly) Albert Hirschman's admonition not to look where everyone else was looking. And so, I looked where no one was looking. I set out with a desire to question my homeland's history — the history I know best, the history that might come to my aid. Perhaps it was to grasp a genetic thread in my reasoning, to see what I had understood wrongly and what rightly — what important things I had missed, and what was keeping me from framing current predicaments more accurately.[109]

And I discovered that, strange as it may sound, the question ought actually to be posed starting from the beginnings of our civilization, and that in my historical foray I would have on my side a villain to mock — my high school education. In other words, from a certain point on, I realized that if I were able to get over at least some of the historical beliefs and prejudices I had unconsciously stored up, I would be able to free myself for new and more solid acquisitions."

13 — By now the reader will have understood that this is the approach I intend to pursue in the following pages, but in this case targeting the Mediterranean and the prewar 'Algerian' formulation referred to above in the first chapter. And how has it turned out? First, I see great agreement on many themes — such as the beauty of nature and of the material civilization of the Mediterranean.

"It is certainly no coincidence," Audisio wrote, for example, "that at least four islands [...] have, in differing forms, the same name: Neapolitan Capri, Majorcan Cabrera, Caprera, north of Sardinia,[110] and Capraia, which stands watch between Corsica and Livorno. It is no coincidence that the two main islands hosting goats [capre], one off Vesuvius and one in the Balearics, at one end of the basin and the other, mirror each other with the same blue grotto. We can see in this a sign of identities, a perfect illustration of the similarities given to us

---

[109] From a methodological viewpoint this is the kind of cognitive interrogation that I learned from Eugenio Colorni in his battle against anthropomorphism (Colorni 1998, 2021; Colorni and Spinelli 2020, Chap. 6).

[110] The one, to be clear, where Giuseppe Garibaldi retired.

by the sea, the symbol of Mediterranean unity." And again, "the olive tree and its oil, the fig tree, the vineyard and the grape explain Mediterranean civilization more than a pile of historical documents or a list of monuments" (Audisio 1935,184 and 171).[111] Perfect!

Nevertheless, concerning other aspects of the Mediterranean scene our judgments diverge, at least in part. Take, for example, an important page from the first book of *Jeunesse* in which the self-styled "barbarian" Audisio seeks (1935, 151)[112] (in the third person) "a human truth in his present gropings. [...] For we have glorified ourselves enough, all of us, in the lyricism of connecting rods and rotary presses; we have sung enough to the rhythm of our steel and dynamo age to allow ourselves to be moved by virtues that are more fleshly, but richer in soul. For me, dispensing with any false shame, I take little consolation in seeing certain aspects of life disappear which I call, in spite of myself, biblical — perhaps because the Eternal [...] has blessed all the work of our hands, or rather because I associate such displeasure with certain kinds of Semitic civilization in which I have lived."

In my opinion, such regret is not sporadic or even accidental in the literature of "la pensée de midi," probably because the latter does not (systematically, consistently) finalize its work. Indeed, if the purpose is really to affirm a Mediterranean homeland against "the worship of force and success through force," then it is important without a doubt to recognize the providential existence of the great reservoir of manual skills of the Mediterranean artisan and peasant tradition. At the same time, however, we have to question *how to productively revive* this tradition so that we can set out toward the fascinating goals we have placed before us.

In other words, instead of listening to the eternal complaints of all the 'bosses' who cannot find apprentices to whom they can pass on their livelihoods, it seems to me more useful to look into how to enhance such skills (both tacit and codified), how to develop them so as to actually make them worthwhile for the new generations, so that we can take the path we desire and really harness modernity for our own ends, however distant.

Is this not the lesson we should draw "from the Mediterranean-born peoples burdened over centuries by successive civilizations"

---

[111] Cf. above, sec. 4 of Chap. 1.
[112] Perhaps, however, by 'barbarian' Audisio meant to allude to 'Berber' as he later clarified with a hint of self-mockery (1954).

who, as Audisio argued (1935, 53), "are always able to come back and be green again, like the laurel near a spring"? And to learn that lesson, is it not important to extend our roots into pre-Roman history?

V

14 — Thinking about central Mediterranean proto-history, "one realizes," as I wrote in *The Game* (2006, 34-5), "that initially, the push toward development came from the south more than from the north. The arrival of merchants and artisans in the Mycenaean period, followed by (once the mysterious half-millennium of antiquity's Dark Ages had passed[113]) Phoenician and Greek colonization probably produced the beginning of an incorporation of the world economy of the time [as Braudel puts it] that tended to favor the southern Mediterranean and to transform it gradually into one pole in the system."

Naturally, we need to take a realistic view of things. The heart of the Mediterranean, Braudel states (1998, 278-279), "was no one's exclusive property. It had room for three systems which sometimes worked together, but more often competed, using force if necessary — namely, the Etruscan, Phoenician and Greek[114] systems (marked, however — especially the latter — by internal rivalries).

"Even the sea was divided up — none of the three systems could gain complete control of it or profit from the advantages which this would have given them." In addition, it was a system based more on barter than money — which made its first appearance in the Greek world but did not establish itself as an essential tool of a monetary economy until the 4th century.

It is in these embryonic conditions that we must try and capture internal *(centrage-décentrage)* oscillations and alternating expansions and recessions. My hypothesis is that the pressure of Phoenician and Greek colonization, with its successes, tended to form, *from the south,* a large and growing hub of the system.

The high point of this trend may perhaps be seen in the rise of Syracuse, especially in the naval victory in 474 of Hiero, tyrant of

---

[113] Cf., above, n. 85.
[114] This is unmistakably the historic dawn of the three great civilizations which, as we will discuss later, have dominated the Mediterranean to this day. (As we know, Braudel — 1998, 248 and ff. — believed that the Etruscans also came from the East by sea and then moved north and south from Etruria. Today, however, the tendency is to consider the Etruscans an indigenous people; and their economic-political system as part of a larger and more diverse Italic world).

Syracuse, over the Etruscans,[115] which, however, according to what little we know of it, was not followed by any real territorial conquest nor, therefore, any stable occupation of the Tuscan metal-mining zone (which had long been coveted). What followed instead was a strong Carthaginian recovery and a long period of instability.[116] Indeed, as I wrote in my *Il giuoco degli déi* (21-22):

> The settlers came in successive waves, in groups, from different *poleis*. They sometimes gave places and cities names from their own homelands, followed a pattern of trade and agricultural settlement and, regarding themselves as incomparably superior to the indigenous population, they founded colonies and sub-colonies etc. All things considered, their behavior was not unlike that of the better-known future colonizers of America [...]
> In another way, though, things happened quite differently. Neither the Phoenicians nor the Greeks, divided by ethnic conflicts along with internal and inter-city rivalries, were able to effectively dominate tine new world, even in the long term. As we shall see, they managed a temporary equilibrium between colonial pressure for expansion and the Italic populations — a "stalemate," however evolutionary and dynamic, within which we might find a thread of Ariadne for some of our own peculiarities. [...]
> With the arrival of the colonizers, there was undoubtedly [...] an increase in wars and disasters. But 'the centuries of unstable equilibrium' also enabled tire interaction and thus more rapid progress of native peoples.[117]

15 — If we now look at the question from the side of the Greeks who, arriving from the sea, founded colonies at many southern Italian locations, we see that we know far too little of their adventure.

---

[115] To celebrate the victory, Hiero donated to the sanctuary at Olympia two Etruscan bronze helmets, spoils of war, carrying appropriate inscriptions dedicated to Zeus as a mark of gratitude for granting him victory over the barbarians — the Etruscans. One of these has long resided in the British Museum, while the more elaborate one, Corinthian style with nose guard and cheek guards and finely engraved with decorative motifs, which probably belonged to an important Etruscan captain, was handed over from Greece to the Region of Sicily in exchange for a small decorative fragment of the Parthenon conserved in Palermo (Domenici 2003).

[116] When Rome, having subjugated the Italic peoples and colonies, emerged victorious from the Punic Wars, the south would finally lose its upward momentum and begin to assume the subordinate historical position we unfortunately know.

[117] In such a way that, as Vidale and Denti have argued, the solution to the impasse would eventually emerge *from within* "a new and variegated form of Greek- indigenous civilization, which would go by the name of Italiote" (1998, 49).

We do know, of course, that the first wave of colonizers came mainly from Chalcis, Eretria, Megara and Corinth.[118]

We know that "in the early days, the sea favored their ventures toward Italy and Sicily," because there is "a coastal current running northwards along the Balkan shoreline. Leaving this current behind in the region of Corfu, it was possible to sail in a day to the opposite Italian coast,[119] there to pick up another current flowing southward. A virtual salt-water river, driving along the coast, it carried ships to the Gulf of Taranto and past the shores of Calabria" (Braudel, 1998, 272).

We also know that since ancient times Magna Graecia has exemplified the economic and political excellence achieved by these colonies. But despite the initial swing of the pendulum in their favor, they ultimately were unable to prevail.

Certainly, we know that many *poleis* here were built more rationally than those of the mother country, and that their extraordinary monumental buildings expressed pride and the ambition to distinguish themselves, even by comparison with Greece itself. In some of them the sciences and arts flourished, and some became a kind of laboratory, where new forms of cultural, political, and civic life were experimented with. In reaction to the routinization of religious life, they even accommodated new ethical and scientific perspectives. ("The origins of the Pythagorean revolt are only too comprehensible," Braudel writes (296). "Taking refuge in 525 in Croton (a sort of Geneva *avant la lettre*) Pythagoras introduced there a reign of justice in which the essential aim was the salvation of souls, not that of the earthly city."[120]

And finally, we know that some of the colonies, hypothetically,

---

[118] "These, Braudel writes (1998, 271), "were the first centers of activity in ancient Greece. The central axis of activity in the country ran from the Euripus channel, where Chalcis is situated, to the Saronic Gulf and the isthmus of Corinth, a slim barrier which from the seventh century was crossed by a *diolkos*, a track with man-made grooves (concave rails) and wooden rollers which allowed ships to be hauled across from the Saronic to the Corinthian Gulf." This first group would soon be joined by the Rhodians and Cretans, the Spartans and Achaeans, the Locrians, Colophonians, Knidians, Trezeni, Phocians, and Terei.

[119] In addition to boasting the earliest Greek settlements, "the Salento," Moscati states (1995, 92, commenting on the exhibition "Ancient peoples of Italy"), "is home to another sort of discovery as well, that of cave habitations by the sea. The greatest and perhaps most significant of these recent discoveries is the 'Grotta delle Poesia' [Poetry Cave] (...) from 'Posia' which means drinking in Greek, because a spring of fresh water once gushed out here. On the walls of the cave a forest of inscriptions, first in the local Messapic language and then in Greek and Latin, indicates the continuity of the cult dedicated to the god Tauthor — a name that the Romans made their own by changing it to Tutor, meaning 'protector.'"

[120] This would be the push to shape the civilization of Croton in its rivalry with Sybaris.

even opened the door to discussion of the political system. Plato's dialogues on democracy and tyranny are, in fact, set in Syracuse.[121] But all this is still not enough to identify a colonial 'style' in the making — one that would be analogous *(mutatis mutandis)* to that of the pilgrim fathers (or conquistadors) in American history.[122]

16 — Let us imagine, however, that something of this kind were to end up emerging from more accurate historical reconstructions. What conclusions could we draw?

The first is a methodological caveat.[123] Comparisons between different historical eras must shun anachronism like the plague. If there is a danger in talking about the genesis of today's America of unwittingly projecting into the past our present living conditions, such a danger is multiplied if we think of an America of that distant time — if we think, that is, of Phoenician and Greek colonization and their influence on the birth of central Mediterranean civilization.

Yet, all we need to do to get on track is to get our thoughts in order. We need only consider, for example, the types of vessels of the time — the fact that at first, timbers were fled simply by knotted ropes[124] (later replaced by wooden joints and nails). Or the fact that, in human terms, the Mediterranean experience was for long stretches of time one of autonomous, poorly connected spaces. "The entire globe," Braudel maintained (1998, 31), "is today far more united as between its constituent parts than the Mediterranean was in the time of Pericles. This is a truth one should never lose sight of."

True? True! Let us therefore think again and repeat our question. Supposing we know a lot more about the Greek colonies (and supposing we explicitly combat our spontaneous tendency toward retrospective anachronism) — what conclusions might we draw?

In an accelerated historical period, as compared to the previous era (but probably not perceived as such), and through a fragmented

---

[121] As known, Plato made two voyages to Syracuse in an (unsuccessful) attempt to inspire Dionysius II with the principles of good government.
[122] Having identified the need, I came across Valerio M. Manfredi's text, *The Western Greeks* (2004). It is "a journey in search of one's origins," which neatly gathers many useful facts and information; but which, inevitably, still leaves us salivating for more.
[123] Here I am following a suggestion from Francesco Guerriero.
[124] An amazing reconstruction of part of one of these early Mediterranean boats built of lotus stalks, pieces of wood and string can be seen in the Hellenic Maritime Museum in Piraeus (Athens). It is a type of small boat still used (and even miniaturized as a souvenir) in the Oristano area of Sardinia.

and unconscious process on the part of its many protagonists, the key point, in my opinion, would remain that of dynamic temporizing, of the sort of action-reaction that allows for the linkage (however difficult and imperfect) of old and new worlds, inherited and indigenous knowledge, culture and lived experience — that allows for the testing (and inventing) of new productive, social, and political forms on both sides of the (complex) barricade.

In a word, a process that launched our civilization on the multifaceted road of *innovation*, an unexpected consequence of the inability of one (the colonizers) to prevail over the other (the Italic peoples) and vice versa.[125]

This is a visual angle that urges us to look at the archaic history of the central Mediterranean in a different way, and one that implicitly suggests we assume a similar attitude regarding other decisive pages in that history — Arab influences come to mind, followed by Spanish, French, etc.

Everywhere, then, for better or for worse, there is a process of fusion of different elements that were initially separate, of cultural learning that is "ingrained" in the socio-historical DNA of our part of the world and that makes it so special — a remarkable reservoir of human capabilities and resources *in potential*.[126]

VI

17 — Therefore, if all of history — as Fernand Braudel liked to say — must serve the purpose of explanation, if "there is no such thing as outdated history" (Gernet) we must cast our minds back three to four thousand years, if not further.

Perhaps it is my interest in the genesis of civilization in the central Mediterranean, or it may be my curiosity about an era that is still little

---

[125] Despite the many attempts of some colonizers and some Italic peoples. By analogy, it is somewhat like what happens in Dankwart Rustow's genetic theory of democracy (Rustow 1970, Meldolesi 1994, Ch. 8), but, as we shall see, with very different evolutionary consequences - unfortunately!

[126] To take just one example. By embedding themselves in the New World and other European countries, our emigrants have long maintained their original physiognomy. At the same time, despite the enormous difficulties they encountered, many of them ended up being very much at home — as if the conditions of adoption actually responded to certain essential characteristics of their origin. Is it reasonable to think that (as the fortunes of the Natuzzis and the Pistorios show) such essential characteristics may eventually be valued even upon their return home to their places of origin?

known. Or perhaps, on the contrary, it is the difficulty of coming to grips with other, more recent aspects of our history. In any case, the fact remains that I find it easier to entertain a helpful, purposeful, and serene attitude with respect to archaic history than contemporary history.

Why did things happen as they did? What were the initial conditions? Evidently, to proceed with our research we must retrace our steps, seeking an answer in the events of the time and in the peculiarities of the colonizers (Phoenicians and Greeks), the colonized peoples, and the Italic peoples who were not colonized — some twenty groups (and more) — and look for a thread that has escaped our grasp.

With this in mind, I thought it might be useful to seek an initial verification of Braudel's analysis in the extraordinary 2000 exhibition on the Etruscans at Palazzo Grassi in Venice.[127]

The main point, as I have mentioned, is that for the Etruscans and other Italic peoples there existed a long process of civilization and learning, through both internal evolution and external influence — first orientalizing (through the arrival of goods and artisans from the East in general), then Phoenicianizing and Hellenizing (through the respective influence of colonizers). It is this learning that prompted the archaeologists in the exhibit to compare the Etruscans to today's Japanese — the people who initiated the "great change" taking shape in the Pacific.

This process of progressive learning allows us to distinguish three main phases in the history of the Etruscans (and other Italic peoples): the incubation phase, the developmental phase of the 8th to 5th centuries (characterized by certain power relations and the emergence of an indigenous aristocratic class) and the decline, lasting more than two centuries.

At this point a doubt crept into my mind. The Phoenician and Greek settlers certainly made a great cultural, economic, political and military impact on overall conditions in the central Mediterranean. But given that we are dealing with human affairs, was there not another side of the coin? What I mean is, didn't the arrival of the colonists also 'alter' the beginnings of the Apennine, Etruscan, etc. civilization discussed above? What if the latter had within it the germs of a different, more favorable evolution than the one that later actually occurred?

As the reader will have guessed, I am referring here to a famous thesis of Carlo Cattaneo's which, as we shall see, has great relevance to our argument.

---

[127] And in the comprehensive catalog edited by Mario Torelli: A.A. V.V. 2000.

"The history of Europe would be quite different," he wrote,[128] "and the people of the north would not have spent so many centuries barren and blind if the Etruscans, starting then, had propagated *their nursery of cities, their generator of cities*, along the Rhine and the Danube. Etruscan rule was different from Roman — federated and multifaceted, it could tame barbarism without extinguishing independence. There was no tendency to aggrandize a particular city, which would be distorted by its very increase and become the material seat of a domain devoid of nationality."

We can sense here the usefulness of a plunge into archaic history — almost as if we wanted to imitate the famous and almost identical figurines that appear (reversed) in tombs in Paestum and in Tarquinia.[129]

Clearly, there is much we can learn from the vitality, versatility, dexterity, learning, and extraordinary inventiveness of these ancient progenitors. Delving into the history of the Italic peoples allows us to 'put our feet on the ground' in the region; today, as then, it helps us appreciate the local level in relation to the 'global.'

18 — Let us take an example, traveling back in time. Where and when can we catch the initial budding formation of our tastes? There is probably no unambiguous answer. Tradition delivers us the somewhat stale idea of the Hellenization of the Romans. But our reasoning rims along a different line of reasoning — that of leaping backwards through the centuries to the history of the Italic peoples.

Though within reach, this field of research is largely unexplored. It is an archaic era in which the formation of regional tastes basically takes place under the influence of people and goods from the East, and then in the relations among the colonizers, the colonized, and the non-

---

[128] Cattaneo, 1844a; now 1957, 799-800. "Note the main (partly implied) concern of the argument. Tire dominant position achieved by the Etruscans in Italy (cf. above, sec. 3 and n. 74) — Cattaneo argues in hindsight — could have allowed them to expand beyond the Alps and thus develop Etruscan "federative and multifaceted" principles along the Rhine and Danube rivers — which, however, did not occur to the great detriment of subsequent European history. (One senses, on the other hand, the Cattanean intention to highlight and enhance the Italian democratic federalist contribution to European construction. A similar attitude can be discerned, for example, in Cattaneo 1861b, now in 1972, 332 ft. [...]. It is this task that continues to be critical — even today, even tomorrow)" Meldolesi 2013a, 37 n.
[129] Like the door, the offering, the clothing, the jewelry, the weapons, the furnishings, the libations, etc., it is a ritual image of a dashing young man who, on behalf of the deceased, performs a perfect head-first dive ... into the afterlife. (The cultural influence, of course, is Greek, but significantly, these tombs belong to two different Italic peoples: the Lucanians and the Etruscans.)

colonized: Bruttians, Sannites, Umbrians, Osci, Sicani, Apulians, Sabines, etc.

Region by region and area by area, it would be of interest to 'fish out' and decipher this or that fragment of taste in the making in widely diverse fields.

Personally, I attempted to perform this exercise on the Etruscan tombs at Tarquinia — on its early orientalizing influences and then on those from Magna Graecia. I reached the conclusion that what I had imagined was indeed the case. That is, that the spark ignites when the external input blends with the vibrant life of the community, creating a fresh, exuberant, unexpected, and expressive result. In the Tomb of the Augurs, the Tomb of Hunting and Fishing, the Tomb of the Leopards and still others, the exercise truly succeeds when this fusion is palpable — when the craftsman-artist accesses "the good and the new." When this reflects taste in the process of formation and feeds it at the same time.

For those who know something about Etruscan culture it must be added that this represents a miracle that comes from suffering. For while tradition initially limited painting to a few decorative features, the later breakthrough of including dining and dancing in honor of the deceased — this extreme attempt to combat pain with pleasure and tragedy with celebration[130] — dramatically presents us with a rare artifact of the primordial genesis of Mediterranean taste.

---

[130] "A visit to the houses of the dead in Tarquinia," wrote Fernand Braudel (1998, 261), "is a joyful pilgrimage, as one goes from one to the next, constantly meeting the colors and sunshine of springtime in Tuscany [Tuscia]. The Etruscans believed in a future life in a quite material sense. The dead person was going to live in the tomb itself, in one or more of these chambers adorned with benches, carved stone friezes, or [...] fresco painting. The whole setting was designed to suggest a private house, to conjure up around the dead person the brightly colored world of the living."

Chapter 3
A Return Journey

The more I try to document pre-Roman history (with readings, visits to museums and archaeological sites), the more clearly I am able to see certain aspects of convergence and divergence of that history with respect to the discovery of America, and the better I can delineate for myself certain key hypotheses. (This in a twofold sense, because the historical genesis of our adventure illuminates what we already know in an unexpected way, and because the study of long-term trends can combine with current events and interventions).

It so happened that I was reminded of an interview that Albert Hirschman did some time ago for a German newspaper on the anniversary of the Holocaust. If you want to build a superior democracy, he argued, you must first admit the wrongs of the past. By unreservedly acknowledging the genocide perpetrated against the Jews, the German people could encourage the American people to recognize their own genocide.

And ourselves? This is a question I would like to address to the Phoenician and Greek colonization in the central Mediterranean.

The answer, fortunately, is that as far as we know there was no genocide, at least on the scale of what occurred in America, either at the beginning (as in Central and South America) or later (as in North America).

Yet Braudel persists in the comparison: "Like modern Europe," he writes (1998, 224), "the Orient of antiquity exported to distant places [through the Greeks and Phoenicians] not only its strengths, but also its inner divisions, its conflicts of interest and its inveterate hatreds. These God-given lands, where the colonizer and the merchant could impose their will without too much difficulty, and where towns sprang up overnight, would eventually be divided up between rival masters, who brought war in their train."

This push toward war was naturally coupled with masculinity, representing a step backwards — indeed, perhaps even more than one — in relations between men and women, compared to Etruscan society, for example. [131]

---

[131] In which, as we know, women had a freer and more elevated role. It is striking that it has taken two and a half millennia of torturous human history to be able to claim that things have

It was a war that initially involved mainly colonial poleis that were rivals for hegemony, which later became a war against the indigenous communities [132] as well and set in motion the complex historical process of action and reaction[133] that would cause great devastation (especially in Sicily and Tunisia) as well as a substantial metamorphosis of Rome itself.

According to Indro Montanelli, in fact, the end of the second Punic war "marked the onset of a transformation in Roman life that was not to prove beneficial to the fortunes of the city. The total of over 300,000 men left on the battlefield had been the pride of Roman agriculture and the army. Four hundred cities had been destroyed. Half the farms had been looted, notably in southern Italy, which indeed has never fully recovered. The Romans of two hundred years earlier would have remedied these afflictions within a few decades. But their successors no longer matched their temperament. What beckoned them now was not work in the countryside, but international trade" (Montanelli 1957,137).

This brings us to the epilogue of our argument, which ties in with Gabriel Audisio's *Sel de la mer*. The fact is, the three Punic Wars between Rome and Carthage (264-241, 219-201 and 149-146 BC) undoubtedly represent a break in continuity, a turning point, which Audisio's *peroratio* in favor of Carthage makes more important in my view than I had instinctively thought.

This is because, among other things, it opens the door to the gradual rearrangement of the Mediterranean more by military than economic means. In fact, apart from the (much harsher) scale of the Punic Wars, I do not think the behavior that had led the Roman army up to that point from victory to victory was significantly different from what it displayed in these circumstances.

The Romans of the Republic had absorbed blood, wealth, slaves, and gods from the populations they had subjugated (while granting their male elites limited autonomy under Roman legal-military authority). But at the same time, they practiced a scorched-earth policy toward peoples who resisted their will by force of arms — to the point of completely destroying their conquered cities, whether indigenous or colonial, and scattering salt on them to signify that they were not to

---

actually changed (and must change still more)!
[132] Cf. Pugliese Carratelli 1996, p.141.
[133] Clearly, this was not a painless process. Like so many things human, Phoenician and Greek colonization was fundamentally two-faced.

be rebuilt. This macabre ritual is alluded to by Audisio in *Sel de la mer* in reference to Carthage.[134]

Today it is discussed, not surprisingly, with reference to the Army of the Russian Federation which, after razing Grozny and Aleppo, invaded Ukraine and massacred the civilian populations of Bucha, Mariupol and who knows how many cities, towns and villages.[135] It is discussed because, here again, it is the issue of the *quantity* of war crimes committed, as well as their horrific quality, that explains the assessment of the conflict.

There was an actual turning point in the case of Carthage and Rome (followed later by other fractures in the Mediterranean area). And it has been remembered *in secula seculorum* in the rhetoric of Romanity and Latinity, even to the point of feeding the myth of Scipio Africanus,[136] and even in the Italian national anthem of Goffredo Mameli, a young poet and hero of the glorious Roman Republic of Mazzini and Garibaldi.

I

1 — I read some time ago in *Il Sole 24 Ore* that, based on factual evidence (and as an effect of the increased attention to the environment typical of our times), the Region of Tuscany was charging a business in the Maremma with polluting a river by dumping arsenic waste

---

[134] Fernand Braudel (1998, 234) explains that to seal the hulls of their ships Carthaginian navigators used bitumen, a kind of natural tar. "The architects in Carthage used it too. The clay walls of the tall houses were often tarred on the outside, and Pliny speaks of their "pitch-covered roofs." Therein lies the explanation for the terrible fire of 146 BC. The Romans would never have been able to burn the city down to ground level had it not been for the highly inflammable bitumen, which is still being found by archaeologists in 'little plaques' in the layer of ashes covering Punic Carthage."

[135] On closer inspection, the only thing missing today in Ukraine is ... the salt! However, if we are going to refer what is happening to the "whirlpool" linking nationalism and imperialism mentioned above (see sec. 10 of the first chapter), the parallelism here is, if anything, reversed. This is because Rome's victory over Carthage marked the advent of Roman nationalism, which was shortly transformed into empire, while the current behavior of the Russian Federation, on the heels of the crisis of European communism triggered by the fall of the Berlin wall looks like the prelude to a possible unraveling of Russia's long imperialist tradition.

[136] According to contemporary legend, Publius Cornelius Scipio known as Africanus, believing that he had been falsely accused of embezzlement, retired to his villa at Liternum in Campania Felix alongside his soldiers. (Veterans who had completed their military service were assigned an agricultural allotment whose 'checkerboard' can still be seen in situ today in aerial photographs.) According to Livy, his tomb in the area originally bore the inscription "Ingrata patria, ne ossa quidem mea habes" (Ungrateful country you will not even have my bones). Later a fragment of it would give its name to the locality and to "Lake *Patria*," nearby.

from its own manufacturing process. The company protested its innocence.

Accordingly, the region commissioned the Science Department of the University of Siena to carry out the necessary inspections. The department's researchers compared the waters of two rivers in the area — the one the company in question had access to and another that was comparable. Finding no trace of arsenic in either of them, they absolved the business. But they did note at the same time that traces consistent with arsenic were (and are) notably present in the area.

What could the cause have been?

Thanks to the collaboration of the Department of History and Archaeology of the same university, the reason for the pollution came to light and an extraordinarily important page in the history of the central Mediterranean returned to the forefront. Well, believe it or not, the reason for the pollution is mining and the production of metal objects, especially weapons, which the area of the metal-bearing hills of Massa Marittima hosted in Etruscan and Roman antiquity, and then again during the Middle Ages, as did Piombino and the island of Elba.

These ancient industries soaked the soil with so much arsenic that when the researchers reached this conclusion, they reversed the order of their reasoning.

Once they had ascertained the cause, they took advantage of the significant presence of arsenic in the soil to plan a new cycle of archaeological excavations which should make it possible to reconstruct and more fully appreciate an extraordinary episode about which we still know too little.[137]

This is an illuminating page in our process of 'civilization.'

Why — it is worth asking — did the Phoenicians and Greeks, who had long known of the existence of the Italian peninsula, decide at a certain point to establish colonies there? In *Memory and the Mediterranean*, Fernand Braudel argues that both of them were first and foremost out in search of metals, even then considered a key to commercial and military power.[138]

---

[137] But what we do know more than justifies a visit to the Lake Accesa archaeological park, the Massa Marittima Museum, the mines, etc. For an overview, cf., for example, Zwingle 2005a.
[138] Cf. in this regard Braudel 1998, 268-75. "Tire piecemeal and apparently haphazard efforts of the Greek cities," he maintains, for example (272-3), "were above all aimed at finding a route to the west (...). The drive westward with little regard for the intervening places is clearly demonstrated by the chronology provided by both archaeology and tradition. (...) Tire Chalcidians and other peoples of Euboea had thus immediately embarked on a race to the

To this end, as we have seen, the Pheonicians positioned themselves in the Iberian Peninsula, but also in the Balearics and in Sardinia. The Greeks, on the other hand, founded their first colonies at Ischia (Pithecusa),[139] around 770 BC[140] Probably, unable to occupy the island of Elba and the Marenima directly, since these were defended by the Etruscans, the Greeks and Phoenicians created 'bridgeheads' to increase their trade from closer by.

2 — This episode is already sufficient to illustrate the "pace" I would like to impart to the present chapter (which — let me be clear — is not meant to represent a simple *'repetita juvant')*. In fact, having by now established a certain outline (however partial, to be re-examined), I would now like to look at its framing — and then gradually add a few more tiles to the discernible mosaic, so as to bring the line of reasoning into more direct contact with the sea, the land, and the common mortals of those distant times.

How? By bathing the analysis in highlights and Mediterranean colors and testing its logic — so as to make it (I hope) more convincing.

Compare, for example, the hypothesis just put forward with the analysis of one of the most distinguished scholars of pre-Roman Italy. Massimo Pallottino, wrote Sabatino Moscati (Moscati 1997, 180-1), "marked out the first millennium on the Peninsula in four major periods: the first including the formative processes of the various ethnic communities up to the 8th century BC, the second characterized by the flourishing of Greek and Etruscan centers on the Tyrrhenian Sea from the 7th to the early 5th century BC, the third marked by the expansion of the eastern Italics and Celts or Gauls in the 5th and 4th centuries BC, and the fourth concerning the unification process under the aegis of Rome."

In my opinion, the first two periods appear more intelligible than

---

most distant places. (...) The pattern is very like that of the Phoenicians, whose first objective was far off Spain."

[139] Pithecusa was founded by settlers from the Euboean cities of Chaicis and Eretria, while Cumae was later established by the Chalcidians. This inaugurated the Greek presence in the Bay of Naples, with the accompanying transfer of their imagery, according to which Typhon (Typhaeus) lies beneath Ischia, the rocks of Ulysses' Sirens are located near the promontory of Sorrento, and Lake Averno represents an entrance to the Underworld...

[140] "Would the Greeks of Chaicis," Braudel wonders (1998, 270), "have been impelled in 770 BC to settle on the island of Ischia in the bay of Naples by purely agricultural considerations? Such a meager reward would hardly have justified such a long voyage. It is, in fact, no coincidence that this first observation post (...) was a vantage point on the Etruscan Sea, within range of Etruscan metal. Metal was a constant concern of the Chalcidians..."

the others. "Regarding the formative period," Moscati writes, "between the 10th and the 8th centuries BC it is characterized by the emergence, on a relatively uniform foundation of prehistoric cultures (Apennine and late Apennine, Villanovan), of regional cultures substantially linked to the territories of historical peoples. (...) Investigation into the origin or provenance of each people has gradually been transformed into a search for ethnic formation, understood as a convergence of movements, overlaps and encounters."

Furthermore, regarding the second period, Pallottino and Moscati put the emphasis on the flowering of Etruscan and Greek centers along the Tyrrhenian. [141] As I have written, the hypothesis of the formation of an unstable *impasse* – between Italic peoples and eastern colonizers in search (mainly) of metals – would in my view lead to a better understanding of the triggering of this flowering, as well as the start of the growth of the southern colonies.

("Broadly speaking," Braudel states (1998, 273-4),[142] "the Greeks and Carthaginians shared occupation of the island [Sicily] from 750 to 650, the former on the east, the latter on the west. But the Greeks' great triumph was to have been the first to seize the hazardous Straits of Messina. It was not a total victory, however, since the Etruscans dominated the Tyrrhenian Sea, and the Carthaginians, by clinging on to the narrow, rugged region of western Sicily, kept possession of an essential link in the route leading 'by way of the islands' to Spain. In a word, the Greeks had designs on the westward route giving access to metals but were unable really to secure it. This did not prevent the colonial Greek cities from flourishing, no doubt because of their extensive and fertile hinterlands. Varro asserts that the grain yield here was a hundred to one. We may remain skeptical, but certainly the threefold

---

[141] "In craft production, in writing, in religious and funerary ideology," Moscati (1997, 181) makes clear, "the Greeks are undoubtedly due a primary influence, which must be taken into account along with both the Etruscan elaboration and influence it exerted in turn, and the profound local autonomies, mostly at the folk level, that are noted and even more so in the later age."

[142] "Carthage, it seems obvious," Moscati (1978) writes, "wanted to drop something like an Iron Curtain in the middle of the Mediterranean, to block the Greeks' way to the West. We can now follow such an Iron Curtain from Cape Bon up through Pantelleria and Malta to western Sicily and Sardinian territory. This is the premise of the clash with Rome." Indeed, "strengthened by these footholds, Carthage exerted hitherto unimagined control over the central area of the Mediterranean, fortifying Cape Bon, settling in Pantelleria and Malta, and dominating the western triangle of Sicily and essentially all of Sardinia. Beyond this area, Carthage's sovereignty over the Mediterranean coast was complete". Accordingly, careful reconnaissance of classical sites and sources recently led Sergio Frau (2002) to identify the Greeks' Pillars of Hercules... as the Strait of Sicily.

triumph of wheat, oil, and wine, in which Diodorus saw the cause of the rapid growth of the Sybarite economy, explains the splendor of these colonial cities.")

Regarding the third period, the ideas are less clear. "Between the 5th and 4th centuries BC," Moscati writes, "there were new and decisive occurrences: the decline of the Tyrrhenian centers of the Greeks and Etruscans, the expansion of the eastern Italic peoples into the surrounding areas, and the penetration of Gallic peoples from the north."

In other words, a confluence of circumstances. But as we have seen, to grasp even a part of this change in the making we must also look at the political-military situation.

3 — Imagine that we are in Carthage. During the period of "unstable equilibrium" this sort of New York *ante litteram* located an arm's length from the Sicilian coast had derived an extraordinary rejuvenation from a series of circumstances: its substantial autonomy, its geographical position, the development of Mediterranean trade, the evolution of the Phoenician world,[143] and the African hinterlands. All this had laid the foundation of Punic power, capable of taking into its orbit many other colonies.

Now, Carthage, as I mentioned, had allied itself with the Etruscans in opposition to the notable expansive push of the Greek colonizers. In 540-535 B.C. this coalition defeated the Greek fleet and expelled the Phocians from Alalia (Corsica). But then, "in 525 Persia seized Egypt and consequently acquired the use of the powerful Phoenician navy which the pharaoh had fitted out. However, Darius was defeated at Marathon (490) and Xerxes at Salamis (480), and in the second of these battles at least, it was the Phoenician ships that were beaten. The same year, the Punic army and navy were crushed at Himera in Sicily, and a few years later the Greeks destroyed the navy of the Carthaginians' Etruscan allies at Cumae (474)" (Braudel 1998, 241-42). Carthage and the Etruscans

---

[143] Cf. above, n. 18 of Chap. 2. As mentioned, Phoenician colonization was supported by a class of arms-makers and merchants who imposed their will on the new world. Now, "recent excavations of the Phoenician colonies of Sardinia have shown that (beginning in the 6th century) Carthage conducted a full-scale 'normalization' in the Phoenician settlements that had sprung up earlier on the island, imposing the cult of its own polyad deity, Tanit, and probably also installing military-type control. The same happened in the Iberian and Mauritanian West where the Carthaginians completely replaced the Phoenicians, recolonizing Cadiz, Tangier and Lixus on the Moroccan Atlantic coast. It was this 'imperial' type aggression, among other causes, that led to situations of open conflict especially with the Greek cities of Sicily" (Manfredi 2004, 72).

thus absorbed an impressive series of defeats.

Now let us turn our attention to Syracuse. Founded by the Corinthians toward the middle of the 8th century, an agricultural colony and later mainly mercantile and military, Syracuse gained a dominant position in the 5th century under the Dinomenid dynasty, begun by Gelon, and ex-cavalry officer and lord of Gela.[144]

Syracuse underwent a substantial process of expansion that led it into victorious conflict with other Greek colonies and with Carthage and the Etruscans, followed by victories over Sicily's Italic populations and over Athens as well. With this last victory, Syracuse "had humiliated the greatest naval and mercantile power in the world at the time, gaining immense prestige (...). Syracuse initiated an expansionist policy that led to the formation of a genuine empire, which for a time extended to almost all of eastern Sicily and a good part of Calabria. Its mercantile ships plied the northern Adriatic in search of new markets, and its imposing battle squadrons kept a good part of western Greece unified for a certain period" (Manfredi 2004, 248). But subsequent history also showed the limits of Syracusan dominance.

In conclusion, because of a combination of factors both within and outside the central Mediterranean (and the various contending camps), what began to come to the fore as early as the 6th century was *power politics*. The temporary, unstable balance between Greeks, Carthaginians, and Etruscans, achieved with the arrival of the colonists, ended up shattered. The Tuscan metal-bearing areas were temporarily occupied. The 'arsenic and old lace' from these districts lost some of their traditional appeal. There was a serious decline in prosperity along the Tyrrhenian coast (favoring the Adriatic) and, Syracuse's 'magic moment' having passed, a turbulent and ominous interregnum ensued.

II

4 — To give you an idea of this I shall once more point to one of the pivotal nodes in the story, the transition from poleis to 'empire' — both because of the importance of the issue itself and because of the economic policy problems of the present that may be mirrored in that decisive hairpin turn. In the thinking of the time, the strengthening of a particular polis generally sharpened its rivalry with multiple cities, which reacted by restoring in some fashion an unstable imbalance.

---

[144] A Rhodian and Cretan colony founded at the beginning of the 7th century.

But, in the 5th century, the victorious war of the Greeks over the Persians and the commercial empire of Athens in the age of Pericles marked what was probably a historical high point.

At the same time, in fact, with the coming of Carthaginian and Syracusan power politics, the city-state system of the central Mediterranean went into decline[145] through processes and mechanisms that we ought to know in greater depth. Then, with the terrible Peloponnesian war between Athens and Sparta, it declined in Greece as well.[146] All this, as I said, created the conditions for an interregnum which led in the end, over the same span of time, to the rise of Rome and the great military adventure of Alexander the Great. In other words, the expansionary drive of the city- state system itself *had finally overflowed* the banks it had up to then been operating within.

I found an intuitive feel for it in the amusing the dialogue imagined by Indro Montanelli (a Tuscan who knew a thing or two about Etruscans) between Tarquin the Superb, the last king of Rome who was exiled (it is believed) in 509 BC, and Porsena, the great Locumon of Chiusi.

The latter, Indro wrote (Montanelli 1957,48-9), "of course had to point out to him that the Tarquins, though of Etruscan blood, had not proved to be good sons when it came to Etruria, having continually tormented it with wars and punitive expeditions (...). But the Superb probably replied to him that at the same time that he and his predecessors were making Etruria Roman, they were also making Rome itself Etruscan, conquering it, as it were, from within at the expense of the Latin and Sabine element that had first dominated it. The struggle had not been between foreign powers, but rival cities that had sprung from the same civilization. Rome, even though youngest, had not tried to destroy them, but rather to reunite them under a single command

---

[145] I am referring here to the Phoenician, Greek, Latin, Etruscan, etc. cities. The misfortune of Etruria, says Braudel (1998, 257) "was to have too many enemies at once and to be itself divided among towns all jealous of their independence — the annual assemblies of the Etruscan cities, at the Faunum Voltumnae on the territory of Volsinii, were religious gatherings, not the makings of a political body. Etruria suffered from the same weakness which caused the disasters of the Greek cities." This is a judgment I intend to come back to.

[146] "But in the long run," Braudel comments (1998, 297-98 and 299-300), "wasn't the fate of Greece fixed in advance? As we know, Greece was fragmented into a patchwork of independent city-states, all of which were liable to fall prey to then often extremes passions. And these passions were in the end fatal." "Athens in 404 opened its gates to Lysander. But neither the victory of anachronistic Sparta, nor the ephemeral rise of Thebes under Epaminondas would throw up any force more capable than Athens of constructing Greek unity. Tire endpoint of the process was the arrival of the great barbarian of Macedonia. Elis coming had been prepared long before."

to lead them to predominance in Italy. Perhaps it had erred, perhaps it had here and there gone a bit overboard, with little respect for their municipal autonomy. But (...) no Etruscan city had ever been sacked. (...) Now, with the republic, what was going to happen? The republic meant the return to power of those loutish, stingy, distrustful, reactionary, and instinctively racist Latins and Sabines who had always harbored a dull hatred for the liberal and progressive Etruscan bourgeoisie. There could be no illusions about how they would treat her. And his disappearance meant the establishment, at the mouth of the Tiber, of a foreign and enemy power (...) which tomorrow could join the other enemies of Etruria and contribute to its demise."

Perhaps Tarquin the Superb's "peroratio" convinced Porsena to unite the Etruscan cities (Sabine and Latin) and defeat Rome *pro tempore*, causing it to take a great leap backward. But he did not convince Porsena to put the superb back on the throne of Rome. Porsena, it appears, only wanted to restore the traditional balances in the system of poleis, so that the issue re-emerged, tragically, over a century later.[147]

5 — One way to ascertain the validity of the argument is to go through it again changing the regional theater it references. For this purpose, I would like to make use of the monumental *History of Calabria* edited by Gaetano Cingari and later by Augusto Placanica, made available to me by the President of the Region of Calabria, Giuseppe Chiaravalloti. In particular, I would like to draw on a fine essay by Mario Lombardo, "Greeks and indigenous people in Calabria: aspects and problems of economic and social relations."[148]

As an antecedent, to convey a sense of the vastness and

---

[147] In the 4th and 3rd centuries, Braudel writes (1998, 257), Rome "engaged Etruria in a war of attrition punctuated by deceptive reconciliations — a kind of civil war. Veil was taken in 396, Volsinii in 265, Falerii in 240. This last date could perhaps be regarded as the final stage in this very complex process of annexation. The Etruscan cities still retained their magistratures, their claims, their aristocracies, their peasant populations chained to the soil like serfs, their harshly treated miners. But Roman civilization and the Latin language were taking a hold that would last for centuries."

[148] The essay is part of the 2nd volume (1st reprint, 2000) and is accompanied by other papers, including "Ethnogenesis and the Political Emergence of an Italic Community: The Lucanians" by Angela Pontrandolfo and "The Archaeology of the Brettii — Evidence and Literary Tradition" by Pier Giovanni Guzzo. I would also include from the first volume (1° reprint 1988) "The Protohistory" by Renato Peroni; "The Archaeology of Archaic Colonies" by Pier Giovanni Guzzo; and Giovanna De Sensi Sestito's essay, "Calabria in the Archaic and Classical Ages: history, economy society."

complexity of the Mycenaean presence in the protohistoric period, "it will suffice to recall that the number of Italian sites touched by Mycenaean trade between the 14th and 12th centuries, and the quantity of artifacts that make up its tangible remains, are no fewer than the traces left by the precolonial and proto-colonial Greek trade of the 8th century taken as a whole" (Peroni 1988, 96).

Apart from the well-known hiatus between the Old and Middle Bronze Ages (the 'dark age' of antiquity), what was about to happen with the arrival of the Greek settlers had thus been prepared for by a very long Mycenaean association and interaction with indigenous peoples — random and intermittent as it had been in practice.

The Greek colonies in Calabria were founded on the Ionian side, mostly, by unmarried men who immediately attached themselves to the local populations.

For better or worse, as a prelude to colony expansion a vacuum was initially created around the polis and its surrounding area for reasons of defense and/or labor supply, often with the establishment of frontier sanctuaries. Then, at a later stage, there was a process of revitalization and re-attraction of indigenous nuclei within the territory the colony controlled (Guzzo 1988, 152, 166, 186).

A colony tended to expand first along the coastal strip that it contested with other colonies and then up the river valleys, finally pushing beyond the mountains on the Tyrrhenian side.

Within the colony, socio-economic and political structures were formed and consolidated by the landed aristocracy, which took over the most prestigious religious, judicial, and political functions and ensured the defense of the polis, mainly through cavalry. It controlled the "assembly of the thousand," while the general assembly probably assumed an advisory or ratifying function (De Sensi Sestito 1988, 230-2).

On this basis, Lombardo's reconstruction highlights an interesting sequence that I would summarize as follows. The formation of Greek cities and the growth of their influence thoroughly permeated the Calabrian landscape from the Ionian coast to the Tyrrhenian coast. The indigenous populations developed a process of adaptation to the new situation.

Sybaris, helped by its location, was more successful than the other colonies,[149] building an 'empire,' which further altered the existing

---

[149] The fertility of the plain of Sybaris explains much of the extraordinary prosperity of this Greek colony. But its wealth was also mercantile since, as Braudel (1998, 274) makes clear,

imbalance among the Greek poleis.

Its destruction at the hands of Croton at the end of the 6th century BC caused a sort of 'implosion' of the Italic community linked to it, which belonged to the Enotri people. New groupings came out of this, also influenced by 'Greater Lucania' in northern Calabria.[150]

In addition, the unscrupulous politics of the tyrants of Syracuse in Calabria, which led to a kind of protectorate over the Calabrian poleis during the first half of the 4th century, favored the emergence, as a backlash, of the pugnacious Brettii (Bruzi) people of the mountainous interior. There was thus a worsening of the region's imbalances which led to the historical decline of the Greek colonial system in Calabria.

Clearly, we are dealing with a complex situation, subject to multiple variations and requiring much investigation. It does reiterate, however, *mutatis mutandis,* the moral of the story mentioned above.

With one additional feature — the decline of the city- state system, which at once facilitated and was accelerated by the rise of Rome and provoked a vast dislocation of political and social forces.

III

6 — At the height of the Risorgimento in the mid-nineteenth century, the death of the widow of Napoleon Bonaparte's brother Lucien — who according to the old aristocracy had 'usurped' both title and property — restored to the Torlonia family possession of the fiefdom of Canino in the upper Viterbo area. Canino includes within its perimeter the ancient Etruscan city of Vulci, conquered in the Republican era by the Romans.

Prince Alexander Torlonia decided to entrust an archaeological reconnaissance of this area (and others) to Alexander François, a military

---

"these cities of the central Mediterranean were above all places of exchange. (...) At this early stage in their history, most western Greek cities were still closely linked to their mother cities, which housed artisans, carriers and merchants. (...) Thus, it seems probable that the fine, multicolored fabrics of Miletus reached Etruria by way of the land routes over the isthmus, from the Gulf of Taranto to the Tyrrhenian Sea. Sybaris owed part of its wealth to the fact that it directed this mule traffic towards its colony in Laos, in the Tyrrhenian Sea. The road, which was quite a difficult one though it went no higher than a thousand meters, could only be used for lightweight precious goods such as woven cloth." Finally, Sybaris exploited copper, iron and silver mines in the interior.

[150] At its maximum expansion, the people of Lucania, having broken away from their Sannite progenitors, dominated a very extensive area, today shared by Campania, Apulia, Basilicata, and Calabria.

man skilled in cartography, who had already made important archaeological discoveries in the Chiusi area.

The thoroughly Italian François, a Florentine who probably had a French ancestor, has gone down in history as one of the greatest grave discoverers of all time.

In order not to disturb the spring agricultural work of 1857, he focused his attention on the Vulci area (which was more abandoned than others), and one fine day (it sounds like a fairy tale) he noticed a row of beautiful oaks lined up on the edge of a travertine gravel slope (part of the Vulci necropolis, located opposite the settlement of the ancient city, as was typical).[151]

François realized from the nature of the soil that the oaks could not have grown there without the existence of landfill soil suitable for their roots, which indicated the presence of a large-scale underground construction to justify the existence of such a landfill.

Digging there, he uncovered the access road to the hypogeum and then a first chamber that turned out to be a crawl space. Disappointed but not daunted, he pressed on — and brought to light one of the most extraordinary art-historical finds of antiquity, the tomb of the Saties, or François tomb.

Its discoverer died shortly thereafter, and the tomb's furnishings were sold abroad. The amazing paintings, which I will discuss, were cut from the tufa wall in 1863. Being the property of the Torlonia family, they were housed (unfortunately) out of the sight of ordinary mortals.

In 2005, however, at the request of Germany, the Torlonia family allowed them to be exhibited in Hamburg. On their return, instead of a repeat of the exhibition in Rome, which could not take place "for contingent reasons," the paintings made a summer stop at Vulci Castle in an exhibition — "Etruscan Heroes and Greek Myths. The François Tomb Frescoes Return to Vulci" — which included a visit to the tomb.

---

[151] "Shortly after the middle of April," François wrote in "Scavi Vulcenti," nel *Bollettino dell'Istituto di Corrispondenza Archeologica* of 1857, "I moved to the locality of Ponte Rotto near the river Flora, and after new explorations I arrived at a hillock of travertine (...) climbed to the top of it (...) and at some distance I spotted a row of ancient oaks, whose verdant foliage was clear evidence of flourishing vegetation which could only derive from very deep soil. Approaching this point, I realized that (...) this row of trees must mark the street of a large hypogeum, and instantly I had called for a helping hand. A little hoeing was enough to verify my thought, and I ordered the corporal to have the entire length of the road uncovered (...). My orders were carried out to the letter, and after two days' work, we were able to deduce the length of the road (underground access to the tomb) as 150 palms, and its width as ten palms."

7 — Nicoletta Stame and I visited both of them with great delight — for a number of reasons.

A historical reason. The apogee of the Vulci Etruscans, like that of the Etruscans of Tarquinia, dates to the 6th century BC. The events that followed were those mentioned above that ushered in an era of instability. During the fifth century a greatly diminished Rome[152] fought on several fronts, facing external threats (from the Volsci, the Equi, the Veienti, the Samnites, and the Gauls) and internal social struggles. From these battles Rome then began to re- emerge, establishing fresh supremacy over the Latin League, conquering Campania and creating a better-balanced social order. This set the stage for a new upward trend on the part of Rome. The François Tomb, which is from the second half of the 4th century, is one of the most extraordinary artifacts of the resistance to such ascendancy.

An ethnological reason. In fact, the rationale for this large underground construction is different from that of other tombs, such as those in Tarquinia or Cerveteri. The protagonist is a leader who had (temporarily) defeated the Romans in one of the many battles of the time and who is portrayed on the right entering the tomb with his nose in the air.[153] He appears to be on the verge of comprehending an omen by interpreting the flight of a bird that a child — or perhaps a dwarf or gnome — is about to release,[154] a bit like the many human beings who, by modern haruspicy, attempt daily to sort out which way the

---

[152] Rome, which under the Etruscan kings had apparently enjoyed considerable hegemonic expansion in central Italy, but which after the unconditional surrender to Porsena alluded to (and the treaties with Carthage and the Latin League that accompanied it) saw its influence reduced to a circumscribed territory on the coast, between Anzio and Fregene.

[153] He is dressed in a *toga picta,* the prerogative of triumphant commanders. Next to it, beyond the side door, there would have been another image of Vel or his father (or another ancestor). If this was the case, the two would be likened by analogy to the two figures painted on the opposite wall — Nestor and Phoenix, two characters from the Iliad who symbolize wisdom and prudence. Also depicted on the right side of the gateway are Amphiaraus and Sisyphus and on the left side Ajax Oileus and Cassandra. Amphiaraus and Cassandra share the gift of prescience; what Sisyphus and Ajax have in common is having committed the sin of pride against the gods.

[154] "But it was only late in the day," Braudel writes (1998, 259-60), "that the orally transmitted *disciplina etrusca,* as the ancients called it, was given a fixed form in the books which so fascinated the Romans of Cicero's time: the *libri haruspicini,* on the art of examining the entrails of victims; the *libri fulgurates,* on the interpretation of thunder and lightning; and the *libri rituales, libri Acheruntici,* an Egyptian-type manual on the voyage of the dead. In a word, it offered a complete system of protective magic for divining (and thus not crossing) the redoubtable will of the gods, for foretelling the future (...). The system gave rise to rules applying equally to the life of individuals and the existence of the state."

wind is blowing.[155]

The main aim of the progenitor of the Saties, as far as we can tell, was not just to help himself cope with the afterlife. His purpose, probably, was to build a large family tomb, a kind of mausoleum, that would anchor his descendants, the Vulcenti and, through them, the entire Etruscan people, in the war against Rome. For this reason, it appears, it was a tomb designed to remain open, and which would be closed forever upon the arrival of the Romans. It clearly distinguishes an inverted T-shaped central area (richly painted and used for welcoming visitors) from the room at the back, reserved for the leader, as well as from a series of side cells (which housed multiple burials), laid out symmetrically to the right and left of the central area.

An art-historical reason. The paintings are of excellent workmanship. They are very different from those of the other tombs. They were likened by their discoverer to paintings of the Renaissance.[156] "Apart from the entrance wall (...), the entire left half of the tomb is reserved for Greek subjects. This is counterbalanced by the right half, which is decorated exclusively with Etruscan themes. But this consideration concerns only the content of the representation, not the form, which is mediated by Greek models, but with of Etruscan clothing. "The paintings," Bernard Andreae argues, "judging from their style, were executed by Etruscan craftsmen between 320 and 310 BC" (Andreae, 2004, 55-6). In content and execution, they seem highly evolved: they may have been based on Greek 'cartoons' and produced by workers trained in Magna Graecia.[157]

The conclusion confirming this reasoning is that it is unlikely that the old leader would have constructed such an elaborate and pedagogical iconographic complex[158] (or would have commissioned the extraordinary paintings of the inverted T) simply to close them off from

---

[155] But, on the contrary, it is apparently a scene from everyday life. Indeed, Cornelia Weber-Lehman, according to Bernard Andreae (2004, 55), "has demonstrated the kinship between this scene and others found on contemporary Attic stelae," in which "parents with young children are depicted playing with swallows being held on a string."

[156] Indeed, in his account of the discovery published in the *Bollettino dell'Istituto di Corrispondenza Archeologica,* François wrote that the tomb's 'vestibule' was "covered with exquisite paintings each fitted with a very clear Etruscan inscription without which one would believe that this tomb had belonged to some other era. Such is the beauty of the paintings themselves that they recall the beautiful age of Botticelli and Perugino."

[157] They in any case show, in both form and content, the extraordinary level of penetration achieved by Greek culture in Etruria before the coming of the Romans.

[158] Note how the contiguous and facing paintings recur in pairs of two by correspondence or opposition.

the eyes of others. Presumably, their dramatic, robust, and blood-drenched force of expression had an explicit main purpose — to spur visitors to get involved in the inevitable war against Rome.

I shall limit myself here to briefly commenting on two large, very gruesome frescoes measuring more than 3 by 1.5 meters which were originally located to the right and left of the large stem of the inverted T in the François Tomb.

The first of these, "The Liberation of Caelius Vibenna by Mastarna[159] and the Triple Massacre of the Etruscan Warriors"[160] was interpreted by our guide as revenge against the three Etruscan warriors, who represent three negative forces (let's call them discord, cowardice, and subjugation), by three Etruscan heroes,[161] enabling the liberation of Vibenna, legendary Vulcente hero — and thus, perhaps, the unleashing of his warrior spirit. The probable meaning, therefore, is

---

[159] Caelius Vibenna, legendary Vulcente hero, gave his name to the Caelian Hill in Rome (Ogilvie 1984, 82-3). Via Celio Vibemra today rims alongside the Colosseum. Mastarna probably became the sixth king of Rome as Servius Tullius, the great reformer of Archaic Rome. "First and foremost," wrote Indio Montanelli (1957, 41- 2), "Servius conferred citizenship on the *libertini,* the children of freed slaves, the *liberti.* There must have been thousands and thousands of people who in that moment became his most fervid supporters. Then he abolished the thirty curias divided according to neighborhoods (the social basis of traditional power), and replaced them with five *classes,* differentiated not based on where they lived, but according to their wealth. The former consisted of those who had at least one hundred thousand asses; the latter of those who possessed less than twelve thousand five hundred. (...) It was these economic differences that also determined the political ones. For while in the curias everyone was equal, at least formally, (...) the classes voted by *centuria,* but these were not equal in number. The first had ninety-eight and in all there were one hundred and ninety-three. So that in practice the votes of the first class were enough to determine the majority. (...) It was a full-blown capitalist or plutocratic regime, giving the monopoly of power to the industrialists, and taking it away from the agriculturalists — that is, the Senate — which had much less money."

[160] This fresco continues (for another 76 an.) on the back wall (to the right of the door that originally led to the *condottiere's* burial chamber) so that the visitor immediately sees the figure of Vibenna.

[161] The three Vulcenti heroes probably represent the entire Etruscan people. The first appears to be blond — possibly of Veneto origin, our guide said. The third is Aulo Vibenna, Caelius's brother. The warriors being killed are from Volsini, Sovana, and a third unidentified Etruscan city. One possible meaning, therefore, is that even Rome (which in the 6th century was a commercial center situated at the far border of Tuscia) had contributed significantly to keeping alive the spirit of Vibenna. But then, clearly, everything changed with the end of the Etruscan kings... In the current culture of today, all trace of this order of problems has been lost. But this was not true during the Risorgimento. We need only recall that in the second half of the 19th century it was common to portray Lucretia, a Roman heroine, with the iron still hot in her hand, having just committed suicide rather than 'give in' to the son of the last king of Rome — Tarquin the Superb. As can be seen, Roman (and Risorgimento) and Vulcan iconography were pitted against each other in armed conflict!

that only the unity of the Etruscan people (gained at the price of bloody battles) could defeat Rome.

Another fresco, "The Sacrifice of the Trojan Prisoners," is an authentic surprise! In the background, two Etruscan gods can be recognized. The female one, Vanth, bears a striking resemblance to an important angel in Christian iconography[162] (which thus has a much earlier historical basis). The male one, Charun, has a blue face (because he deals with corpses) and is holding the large wooden hammer that opens the gates to the afterlife.

But, in the foreground we actually find Achilles who, in honor and memory of his friend Patroclus and under the consenting gaze of Agamemnon, is killing a Trojan prisoner. Finally on the right two other characters from Greek mythology (Ajax Telamonius and Ajax Oileus) are leading two other Trojan prisoners to their death.[163]

The drama is thus served. The Romans claim to be descended from Aeneas, and therefore from the Trojans. Well then, "Etruscans, remember that the Trojans were beaten by the Greek coalition," is *condottiere* Vel Saties's message to the Vulcenti and the Etruscan people.

The main implication was that the Romans could be beaten by the Etruscan coalition (possibly allied with others). The second was — if we don't do to the Romans what the Greeks did to the Trojans, the Romans will do it to us.[164]

---

[162] The comparison with Renaissance art comes to mind especially here, if anything (it seems to me) with Fra Angelico (or earlier, Pietro Cavallini) ...

[163] According to Bernard Andreae (2004, 52), "the success of this motif might be explained by the public execution of three hundred and seven Roman prisoners in the forum of Tarquinia. The event dates to 358 BC and is linked to clashes over supremacy in central Italy, a question that at the time particularly concerned Tarquinia and Rome. Since the Romans declared themselves descendants of the Trojans, Etruscans would have equated the mythical sacrifice of the prisoners on the tomb of Patroclus with the act of revenge for their own fallen."

[164] Finally, two paintings placed to the left and right of the entrance of the stem of the inverted T complete the series of frescoes. One depicts the mutual killing of Eteocles and Polynices as they fought for supremacy over Thebes, while the other shows the overpowering of a Tarquin of Rome by a Marcus Camillus of Vulci. "It could be a case of desiring to express visually the belief that the Etruscans of Vulci and Tarquinia were in reality brothers, but ones who, in the primordial stages of Rome — conveyed here on the mythical level — were in fact rivals. However, while the Greek brothers killed each other, events played out differently among the Etruscans." Vibenna, in fact, as mentioned, played a leading role on the Caelian Hill, and Mastama (i. e. servant of his Master, Vibenna) perhaps became Servius Tullius.

IV

8 — Now back to where we started. The systematic destruction unleashed by the Russian Federation in Chechnya, Georgia, Syria, and now in Ukraine re-introduces from a different angle the question of nationalism, imperialism and more generally the violence that has been, is now, and will unfortunately still be associated with human life unless humanity itself decides to extricate itself from it, perhaps in stages.

To seek insight into the matter, it therefore seems useful to me to once again take up the *ab initio* argument — not to reconnect with a hypothetical golden age that never existed, but to pinpoint at birth (as far as is humanly possible) some at least of the, often unfortunate, events that finally pushed our ancient ancestors down the nationalist and imperialist paths that are often considered foundational to the Western world.

In fact, from what I have been able to ascertain so far it is undoubtedly true what "la pensée de midi" maintains, namely, that in the Mediterranean there is a repository of civilization that has formed gradually, as if it were the product of successive geological eras, onto which humanity should be able to graft extraordinary positive developments, ones indeed quite different from what we have known so far.

But this would mean being able to control and gradually de-fang the nationalist and imperialist hegemony and aggression that have long fed each other with their rivalries, and in the end "defusing" the typical temptation to dominance that inevitably implies a rationale of subordinating others to one's own will. As we shall see below, on both the large scale and the small and in thought as well as action, the key requirement then becomes knowing how to move *against the grain* with respect to these disreputable age-old impulses.

The observations of 'la pensée de midi' on how to live, on current everyday life, on natural, human and artistic beauty, on moderation, on pleasantness, on the regenerative Mediterranean Sea, etc., turn out to be an extraordinarily useful 'grounding' for our search for such a way out — both in themselves and (as we will see better later on) as an alternative to so-called modernity, with its maddening rhythms, loss of meaning in life, and tendency to sink into the void of melancholy and resentment....

But how to reconnect our scattered branches to that end — we Italics, we Greeks, we Phoenicians, and above all we human blends of so much history? It is not at all simple. Concerning Carthage, Audisio showed us the interesting avenue of the cultural polemic, which, however, as we have seen, requires more detailed knowledge than it might at first glance seem. The fact is, the destruction of Carthage represents perhaps the culminating event in a very broad process affirming the power politics and ascendancy of republican Rome, which would pave the way for imperial Rome.

9 — The destruction of Carthage had far-reaching consequences, even over a great span of time, for the peoples that Rome subdued (and then allowed to survive in subordination within its system). In the sphere of the central Mediterranean alone, this was true for the Italic peoples (the Etruscans especially), and it was even more true for the Phoenician colonies in Tunisian, Siculo-Western and Sardinian lands (on whom the typical Roman "Vae victis!" came down first). And also, inevitably, for the former Magna Graecia.

This last consequence is a factor that I had initially underestimated, but which at some point spontaneously 'registered' in my mind. I was studying the development of German culture in the 18th to 19th centuries.[165] I noted that Winckelmann the great expert on ancient sculpture, had stayed for a considerable time in Rome, where he invented the first archaeological museum in human history on the Capitoline Hill and wrote extensively on Greek (not Magna- Greek!) sculpture as revived by the Romans, thus creating a pro-Hellenic fashion in Germany that played a major role in the great German cultural awakening. I also learned from reading his *Italian Journey* that Goethe had traveled as far as Palermo, visited the Magna-Greek temples of Segesta and Agrigento along with the spectacular theater at Taormina, and had pronounced, "Sicily is the key."

Then, however, upon returning to the continent, as they say in Sicily, he followed Winckelmann in attributing to Greek (and not Magna-Greek) culture a founding role in the new cultural construction — on which the Greco-Roman legacy (with a German flavor) was later regenerated. This was a traditional sort of behavior which in a certain sense ended up compromising "everybody."

What I mean is that on this point very few intellectuals, even the

---

[165] "At the end of the 18th and beginning of the 19rth centuries," writes Cambiano (2022,12) "there emerged in Germany a new image of Greece as a world of beauty in which philosophy also found its place and could flourish as an expression of the splendid public life of the Greeks."

best of them, have measured up culturally to the need — in my opinion perfectly well-founded — to 'give Magna-Graecia its due.' What prevailed instead was the vulgate of 'imperial Rome' which found it convenient after the conquest to attribute the entire Greek 'heritage,' including what Rome had destroyed (and in part absorbed) in Magna Graecia, to the Greek mother country — if not to Athens alone.

Thus, a tradition was formed and *invariably repeated*[166] that viewed Greek philosophical, artistic, political, and scientific thought in the abstract, broadly linking it to the Greece washed by the Aegean Sea. Magna-Graecia disappeared from the scene and became for most people a "sleeping beauty," if not an actual question mark.[167]

10 — Of course, since metropolitan Greece was then occupied by 'the Turk,' neither Winckelmann nor Goethe could verify their surprising conclusions in the Hellenic field. They succeeded, however, unintentionally (and at a great distance in time) in instilling in me a doubt that a 'substitution of protagonists' had *ipso facto* taken place. Because if Braudel was right to argue that between the 10th and the 6th centuries a central Mediterranean 'America' had been discovered by Phoenician settlers (on one side) and Greek settlers (on the other), the inevitable conclusion is that, at least initially, it was the latter (and not the Greeks of Greece) who had influenced the Romans.[168]

Manfredi (240) writes, for example, that "the success of the Greek colonization of Sicily "was of such exceptional import that beginning in the fifth century, the fortunes of Sparta and Athens, the major powers of the motherland, also seemed to be linked to those of Sicilian Greekness — somewhat like what happened to the European powers vis-a-vis America in the first half of the twentieth century and during the two world wars. This is particularly true of Syracuse and Agrigento, which

---

[166] The reason is probably that by separating it from the glory of Rome, such a pro-Hellenic tradition allows it to be used for other purposes — usually similar (such as those of the Holy Roman Empire, the Reich, the Tsarist regime, etc.), but also opposite, such as that of Albert Camus to which we will return in the next chapter.

[167] While they have not had the cultural strength to reverse this unjust rule, there are numerous — but scattered — site-specific studies, that take exception to it, such as those on Calabrian Magna Graecia referred to above in Sec. 5.

[168] Starting with the term 'Greeks.' Indeed, "if nowadays we call the Hellenes Greeks, it is because the Romans called them Graii. But if the Romans did call them this, it is only because the Hellenes of Cumae called themselves Graikoi. This name in fact distinguished only a few maritime peoples of Boeotia and the neighboring coast of Euboea, but the Romans mistakenly transposed it as universal, transmitting it down to us" (Manfredi 2004, 85).

became true superpowers — such that for a time Syracuse was the largest city in the known world and Agrigento, perhaps, the richest." (And it is also true that some of the greatest philosophers, mathematicians and scientists, Greek in culture and language — such as Empedocles in Akragas (Agrigento), Pythagoras in Croton and Archimedes in Syracuse — lived and worked in Magna Graecia).

At this point my initial doubt had put down roots. Luckily, my high school education came to my aid. What I mean is, it seemed to me highly unlikely that such a curious 'quid pro quo' would have been invented by the illustrious German intellectuals named above. Were they not perhaps using a pre-existing, ready-made 'intellectual mold'? Could the idea of the importance of Greek culture to Rome have been a product of traditional Roman peasant values? Not at all! In all likelihood it had sprung from the transitional cultural climate that led to the Empire — from the works of Lucretius, Cicero, Seneca,[169] and above all, Horace.

It is a story that is almost unbelievable. The founding legend of Rome, as we know, goes back to the Trojan War — that is, to the revenge of the Trojans (posthumous though it was, through Aeneas and his descendants) on the besieging Greeks, led by Achilles, Hector and Menelaus.[170] Hence Virgil's *Aeneid*. At the same time, however, Horace argued that, though "conquered, Greece captivated its savage conqueror [Rome], and introduced the arts into agrarian Latium"[171] (a 'classical' proposition, repeated a thousand times, and not surprisingly adored by our high school professors).

---

[169] Probably — this is my hypotheses — it was precisely the patrician desire for self- aggrandizement (and at the same time to glorify the eternal city and its myth-making) that fostered the rise of an artistic, literary, philosophical, and scientific movement that drew on metropolitan Greece — which was often idealized to the point of implicitly and silently absorbing within it, in the imagination of Roman intellectuals, the contributions of Magna Graecia and other Greek colonies. "It was above all the gaze from the outside, projected by the Romans," writes Cambiano (2022, 11), for example, "especially Lucretius, Cicero and Seneca, which recognized that although philosophy was a Greek thing, it was now available to all, including the Latins — hence the basis for establishing the notion of 'ancient/ which included both Greece and Rome, and a first step toward the integration of Greek philosophy into the body of a Europe that was heir to ancient Rome".
[170] The legend of descent from Aeneas (and thus from the Trojans) ipso facto (and with good reason) places Rome in an antagonistic position with respect to the Greeks. This is generally glossed over in the Italian schools (but showed up at the time even on Etruscan tombs — cf. above, sec.).
[171] "Graecia capta ferum victorem cepit, et artes intulit agresti Latio".

11 — Whether it was lined up, then, on the Trojan or the Greek side in neo-imperial Rome, Magna Graecia ... had by this time disappeared, and so it has remained *'in secula seculorum,'* despite the Renaissance.

If we accept, then, Braudel's thesis of the discovery of an America in antiquity, we must as a consequence accept the fact that Greek culture is, in essence, a (partial) 'substitution of the subject under study.' A 'swap,' in other words, of Syracuse, Sybari or Naples, for Athens, Corinth or Sparta (as if in modern America instead of New York, Boston or Philadelphia one were to look to London, Manchester or Newcastle). It is a 'switcheroo' (said with a hint of irony) that became established in antiquity with the rise of the Roman empire, and one that is heavily tinged with Rome's military ascendancy over Magna Graecia. It is sleight of hand facilitated by the sequence of events. This is because Syracuse's victory over Athens (with the help of Archimedes' famous burning mirrors) did not mark the beginning of the colonies' war of independence from the mother country (modern American style).

Instead, as we have been taught since we were little, Rome established its domination over other indigenous and colonial groupings, which gradually lost their independence — cultural and otherwise. It was this rapid incorporation (in successive waves) that underlay Magna Graecia's institutional dissolution, and evidently the regional reorganization desired by Augustus. (Although this plainly did not mean the disappearance of the amazing temples at Agrigento, Segesta, Paestum etc., or archaeological areas of Siracusa, Locri, Crotone, Sibari, Metaponto etc. Nor the disappearance of Magna-Greek influence at the popular level, in ways of thinking, in mythologies[172] — even to the point that only a few years ago there were still small southern localities where ancient Greek was spoken, perhaps the descendant of the language originally brought to the central Mediterranean by the colonizers).

This is an aspect, then, that for our part of the world needs to be restored in its historical reality, to enable (at least in part) the start of the journey to the roots of the problem we are so passionate about — the search for a human escape route from the national-imperialist mindset.[173]

---

[172] Which each colony or group of colonies adapted to their own conditions and developed further — both in Campania, (cf. above, n. 3), and in Sicily (now documented in detail by Guidorizzi and Romani's specialized "mythological guidebook" — 2022). These are intangible cognitive aspects that 're-emerge' from central Mediterranean culture and will play a major role in its much-needed posthumous reconstruction.
[173] This is an intellectual exercise to be developed in both directions. For while it is true that

Because abandoning to its fate the so-called Greco-Roman heritage as the basis of our civilization concerns not only the Roman and therefore Latin side of the equation (as Audisio suggests), but it also concerns the Greek side as well.

It means valuing the technical thinking (of Pythagoras and Archimedes) alongside the philosophical thought (of Empedocles and Plato) and the, often reproduced, artistic thought[174] of pre-Roman Magna Graecia, so as simultaneously to seek dialogue with the Phoenician colonies and more generally with the Hebrew-Semitic world[175]

And not only that — the reverse seems to me also to be true. That is, opening the door to a dialogue with the other shore of the Mediterranean is also indispensable for raising the value of our own shore, in its original components — Italic, Phoenician, Greek, Gallic, Teutonic — and their numberless creative "mixes." Such a re-evaluation of the central Mediterranean might also pave the way for its gradual spread — to the Mediterranean, to the people drawn to it, to Europe and Africa, and eastward to the Middle East, then to Latin America and so on.

V

To summarize — in discussing the pre-Roman history of the central Mediterranean several times from different angles, I hope to have lent weight to the idea the Punic Wars between Carthage and Rome did indeed mark a watershed, a turning point.

The consequences of this earthquake have turned out to be deeper, broader, and longer-lasting than is generally believed, for a number of

---

in the case of Carthage and Magna-Graecia it is a matter of bringing cultural judgment back into line with reality (since the former was unjustly slandered and the latter dumbed down and disregarded), in modern times the reverse relationship has manifested itself as well. So that, for example, the ideals of the great revolutions, their federalist projections, international institutions, etc., have not yet in practice succeeded in getting to grips with nationalist and imperialist rivalries — even though (another paradoxical contrast pointed out to me by Nicoletta Stame) such ideals are often solemnly affirmed in legal terms originally invented...by the Roman Empire.

[174] It is well known that in the Greek and later the Roman world there was no obsession with the original work as in the modern world. So that (unless we want to fall into the usual anachronism) it is not advisable to go searching up and down the Peloponnesus for the original work (perhaps in order to identify the author who supposedly invented it).

[175] Western philosophical culture has long nurtured a sort of 'reductio ad unum.' Perhaps it is precisely the *inversion* of this way of thinking — and the consequent revaluing of the experiences of the different Italic peoples, the many Greek and Phoenician colonies etc. - that will help us out of our suffocating "Nessus shirt" so that we can build the future.

reasons. The severity of the vertical rupture was as if between two "tectonic plates" with respect to the previous world, and the characteristics of the diverse coalitions that faced each other in such acts of war were also of particular importance. And then the outcome, which gave the Romans the keys to the rich Mediterranean upmarket trade network, along with the prospect of exercising dominance *'a part entiere'* over a vast area. Not to mention the subsequent cascade of consequences deriving from it in the complex and tortured historical process reaching down to ourselves.

All right, the reader will be thinking, but why this interest — now? Because we are thinking about the roots of our civilizations in order to address the problems of the present with greater awareness. Because the idea of rehabilitating the vanquished (let's call them that) of both camps carries with it a desire (and perhaps possibility) to kick-start their Mediterranean activities, to engage them, *mutatis mutandis,* in an alternative, unprecedented perspective — while keeping in mind the successive geological eras that have successively favored places and peoples along the road to modernity and democracy. This is the pole star, the beacon, the phoenix (the ancients called it) that we must not lose sight of.

Justice for the Semites and the Jews. Justice for the Magna-Greeks. Justice for the Etruscans. Justice for the indigenous peoples of the African side as for those of the European side of the Mediterranean. It is also a way of gradually identifying the many potential hotbeds of rebellion that exist with respect to the present state of affairs, giving priority to those that show more practical ability, willingness, and foresight in a process that may even territorially alter their zeal.

This is precisely what has happened over time in our own limited experience, which has been shifting its focus southward from its native Campania to Calabria and Sicily; and which does not rule out the future possibility of crossing the long-contested channel that separates us from Africa.

PART TWO
FIGHTING BACK

CHAPTER 4

European Pride, Mediterranean Pride

> "A nihilist is not one who believes in nothing, but one who does not believe in what exists."
> Albert Camus, 1951 (now 1962, iii, 201).

I

In 1943-44, Albert Camus wrote "Letters to a German Friend" — four letters to a young imaginary German soldier steeped in Nazi propaganda.[176] He published several copies in France after the Liberation and then in Italy. Instrumental in this last decision, as he made clear (1962, iv, 381-382), was his "long-standing desire to contribute, insofar as I can, to removing the stupid frontiers separating our two territories."[177]

These were pages, Camus added, that were meant to be read in secret. Their purpose was to bring some clarity to the blind struggle we found ourselves in, to make it more effective. "When the author of these letters says *you*, he doesn't mean 'you Germans' but 'you Nazis.' When he says *we*, this doesn't always signify 'we Frenchmen' but 'we free Europeans'." He continues: "I am contrasting two attitudes, not two nations, even if, at a certain moment in history, these two nations personified two enemy attitudes. To repeat a remark that is not mine, I love my country too much to be a nationalist. And I know that France and Italy would stand to lose nothing, quite the contrary, in opening up to a more inclusive society. But we are still a long way off, and Europe is still being torn apart."[178]

---

[176] These are texts, as Roger Grenier wrote (1987,165), which "against the blind Nazi mystique of force and the state, offer the values it is worth living, fighting and dying for." [After working with his friend Pascal Pia at *Alger-Republicain*, Albert Camus had been forced to emigrate to France because, at the outbreak of war, that newspaper had been suppressed. Hence, following an initial period in Paris as the editorial secretary of *Paris-soir*, his anti-Nazi wanderings between different locations, and between numerous journalistic, editorial, and pedagogical commitments (while he had not been able to participate as a volunteer in the French armed forces because he was ill with tuberculosis), ensued. Camus finally joined the Resistance in November 1943.]

[177] An implicit statement of sympathy for Italians that calls to mind his 1937 statement from *La nouvelle culture méditerranéenne* — cf. above, sec 8, chap. 1.

[178] From this perspective, Camus concludes, his "Letters to a German Friend" are "a document

Indeed, the theme of Europe plays a significant role in these writings. Not least because "from the moment during World War II when the German armies were forced to go permanently on the defensive, national-socialist propaganda embraced and began to massively disseminate the formerly despised idea of Europe, presenting the German Reich as the last bastion capable of protecting the European fortress from the onslaught of Asian Bolshevism, and declaring the Nazi war of conquest and extermination the West's Last Crusade" (Lepenies 1992, 47-8).

Also in this regard, Camus indignantly wrote in the third letter (the one dated April 1944) addressing his fictitious "German friend" (Camus 1962, iv, 396), that "we no longer speak the same language; our Europe is not yours. [...] And that idea of Europe that you took from the best among us and distorted into your own hateful version needs all the power of heartfelt love to preserve in us its youthfulness and strength."

"Europe," he added further on, "is a home of the spirit where for the last twenty centuries the most amazing adventure of the human spirit has been going on." Our Europe "is a joint adventure that we shall continue to pursue, despite you, with the inspiration of intelligence." [...] "Sometimes [...] I happen to think of all the places in Europe I know well. It is a magnificent land molded by suffering and history" (ivi, *397*, 398-99).[179]

1 — Another interesting text for our purposes is the fourth letter, from July 1944, which heralds the allied victory and opens with an epigraph from Obermann: "Man is mortal. That may be but let us die resisting; and if our lot is complete annihilation, let us not pretend that this is justice!"

In a word, as Grenier (166), observed, "suddenly rebellion flashes." This letter, in fact, "is the most important in relation to Camus' work. [...] It already contains the complete doctrine of *La Peste* and *L'homme révolté*." In a way, I would add, it lets the evolution of Camus' main interest shine through — from the absurd (like the German invasion) to rebellion against all injustice, involving the resolute affirmation (and

---

in the struggle against violence" - a perspective that already heralds *L'homme révolté* (1951).
[179] "At the time," commented Roger Grenier (1987, 165), "rare were those who [like Camus] still dreamed, or already, of Florence, Krakow, Vienna, Prague and Salzburg as to 'one face which is that of my greatest homeland'."

preservation) of human values: justice, hope, solidarity, the centrality of women and men, *le bonheur*,[180] respect, the banishment of hatred, and the courage of rebirth.[181]

At the end of 1943, at the suggestion of Pascal Pia and Claude Bourdet,[182] Camus was co-opted into the editorial staff of *Combat*,[183] and gradually took over its reins with the task of ferrying that now grown-up and authoritative newspaper into liberated France. During and after the liberation of Paris, that is, from August 21, 1944 (and until June 3, 1947), he published in it numerous articles and editorials in which he was maturing his views on justice and injustice, measure and disproportion, revolt, and violence, etc.

Having exhausted the *Combat* experience (which finally ended with the emergence of some political dissent within it), Camus felt freer to follow his inspiration unhindered. He met the poet Rene Char and became friends with him. He wrote in 1948 that Char "is new. But his superb newness is ancient. It is that of the sun at noon, of living waters, of the couple, of natural mystery, of bread and wine and inexhaustible beauty. [...] The only living one among the survivors, he takes up in a new way the rough and rare tradition of meridian thought. Char was born in this light of truth."[184]

Camus, wrote Domenico Canciani (2023, 185), "discovers himself in perfect harmony with his friend [...]. In Char he identifies the sketch of that man in revolt on whom he has already begun to reflect. And it is from him that he will have the necessary support to complete his 'difficult navigation,' his theoretical masterpiece, a source of suffering, ostracism, solitude."

---

[180] "To rejoice in the calls of birds in the cool of the evening"; "to cherish in the heart the memory of a happy sea, a hill never forgotten, the smile on a dear face."

[181] Camus' fourth letter to his so-called "German friend" (1962, iv, 399) concludes with the following words: "In short, you have chosen injustice, you have placed yourself with the gods. [...] I, on the contrary, have chosen justice, to remain faithful to the earth. I still believe that this world has no higher meaning. Yet I know that something about it does make sense: it is man, for he is the only being who demands to have one."

[182] "It is thus," wrote Bourdet (1975, 314; quoted in Canciani 2023, 122), "that Camus's name was and will remain closely associated with *Combat*, for which, in the final phase of the underground, he wrote most of the editorials...."

[183] "A newspaper, Canciani recently wrote (2023, 114-15), to which even today we still look with wonder and admiration."

[184] "It is profoundly instructive," the passage continues (published in 1959 as an introduction to the German edition of Char's *Poesies*; cited in Canciani 2023, 185), "that [Char's] words of healing come from Provence that is tender and haughty, funereal and lacerating in its evenings, young as the sun in its hands, and patiently guarding, like all Mediterranean countries, the sources of life to which exhausted and neglected Europe will one day return to drink."

And finally, within a small literary collection entitled *L'été*, the expression "pensée de midi" flowed from the pen of Albert Camus in 1948 at the end of a short essay, "L'exil d'Hélène."[185] This is a piece of writing that brings together some of the appealing characteristics that had already emerged here and there, unobtrusively, in the author's vast literary and journalistic output of the 1930s and 1940s[186] — such as beauty (even in despair), a sense of limits, the (Socratic) knowledge of not knowing, balance and harmony, nature, the sea, the hills, evening meditation, the landscape, freedom, respect for ancient virtues such as friendship.

And in addition, under the title "Thought at the Meridian," the same topic, from a different point of view, concludes one of Albert Camus' most challenging books *L'homme révolté* [published in English as *The Rebel*], to which we must now turn our attention.

2 — By then a famous writer (mainly for his absurdist trilogy[187]), Camus published this long essay on rebellion (Camus 1951, now 1962, iii, 128-437), which naturally considers the experience of the recently concluded world war, and the political-cultural debate that followed.

Let me be clear that the observations that follow make no claim to being an overall assessment of this poetic-philosophical book, so courageous and often misunderstood (much less Camus's work in general, which I know only in part). I am merely seeking to identify within the fabric of this author's work a guiding thread (regarding "la pensée de midi"), to which I can then link my own particular reasoning.

If I am not mistaken, this will require that I initially gloss over the heated polemics that followed the publication of the book (and which today, after the Russian invasion of Ukraine, appear downright absurd to us, and even 'revolu a jamais'), and try instead to reconnect with the author's original intentions — especially those which, starting with the evocation of the "prodigious history [...] of European pride" (Camus 1951; now 1962, iii, 141) eventually lead him to his presentation of "Thought at the Meridian."

---

[185] "Ô pensée de midi, la guerre de Troie se livre loin des champs de bataille! Cette fois encore, les murs terribles de la cité moderne tomberons pour livrer, 'âme sereine comme la calme des mers', la beauté d'Hélène." (1962, ii, 97).

[186] Cf. for example the other essays in *L'été* and those in *Noces* (ibid. ii).

[187] *L'Etranger* (1942), *Caligula* (1944), and *La Peste* (1947).

3 — Rebellion is a dimension of present-day life. "Insurrection," Camus wrote (151), "is certainly not the sum total of human experience. But the controversial aspect of contemporary history compels us to say that rebellion is one of man's essential dimensions. It is our historical reality. Unless we ignore reality, we must find our values in it."

"Rebellion arises from the spectacle of the irrational coupled with an unjust and incomprehensible condition. [...] Two centuries of rebellion, metaphysical and historical, present themselves for our consideration. Only a historian could undertake to set forth in detail the doctrines and movements that followed one another. The following pages," he continues, "do no more than set down some historical landmarks and a provisional hypothesis. It is not the only hypothesis possible; moreover, it is far from explaining everything. But it accounts partly for the direction, and almost wholly for the frenzy of our time" (140-41).

As is well known, this is a thematic book. The author points out at the beginning of the first chapter that rebellion rests on a "categorical refusal to submit to conditions considered intolerable and on the confused conviction that a position is justified, or rather that, in the rebel's mind, he or she 'has the right to...' Rebellion cannot exist without the feeling that somewhere, in some way, you are justified" — without appealing, that is, even silently, to some value (143).

The problem (discussed at length for over three hundred pages) is that when a revolt exceeds a certain measure, as it often does, it degenerates into violence and murder.[188]

"I rebel, therefore we exist" - Camus wrote (152). "In order to exist, man must rebel, but rebellion must respect the limits that it discovers in itself — limits where minds meet and, in meeting, begin to exist. Revolutionary thought, therefore, cannot dispense with memory — it is in a perpetual state of tension. In contemplating the result of an act of rebellion, we shall have to say, each time, whether it remains faithful to its first noble promise or whether, through lassitude or folly, it forgets its purpose and plunges into a mire of tyranny or servitude."

---

[188] Of course, to understand the rationale of something that at a distance might look like a full-blown obsession requires that we go back to the cultural climate of the time — among other things characterized by a steady stream of disturbing news about political trials, police measures, 'purges,' and concentration camps in the Soviet Union (whose tragic dimensions, however, were not known).

II

4 — Therefore, whether (sometimes) confused in their intentions and initial values, Camus considered rebellions to be indispensable and positive. But they actually play out under a sword of Damocles — that is to say, under the great danger of their tragic *'perversion.'* This threat is discussed in the text concerning "Metaphysical Rebellion"[189] (second chapter), "Historical Rebellion" (third), and "Rebellion and Art" (fourth).

"The Sons of Cain" is the author's label for those who end up taking the metaphysical rebellion to extremes. That is, to "absolute negation" (as in Sade[190]) to the "revolt of the dandies" in Romantic literature,[191] to Ivan Karamazov's "rejection of salvation,"[192] to the "absolute affirma-

---

[189] "Metaphysical rebellion is the means by which a man protests against his condition and against the whole of creation. It is metaphysical because it disputes the ends of man and of creation." "An act of rebellion on his part [the rebel] seems like a demand for clarity and unity. The most elementary rebellion, paradoxically, expresses an aspiration to order. This description can be applied, word for word, to the metaphysical rebel. He attacks a shattered world to make it whole. He confronts the injustice at large in the world with his own principles of justice. Thus, all he wants originally is to resolve this contradiction and establish a reign of justice" (153, 153-54).

[190] "Intelligence in chains," Camus wrote (167-68, 169 and 172) "loses in lucidity what it gains in intensity. The only logic known to Sade was the logic of his feelings. He did not create a philosophy; he pursued a monstrous dream of revenge. Only the dream turned out to be prophetic. His desperate claim to freedom led Sade into the kingdom of servitude; his inordinate thirst for a form of life he could never attain was assuaged in the successive frenzies of a dream of universal destruction. In this, at least, he was our contemporary." "His logic leads him to a lawless universe where the only master is the inordinate energy of desire." "But to desire without limit comes to accepting being desired without limit. License to destroy supposes that you yourself can be destroyed. The law of this world is nothing but the law of strength; its driving force the will to power."

[191] Remember the tradition of the "accursed poets," the *poète maudit*? Well, "for the romantic a supreme value is attached to frenzy. Frenzy is the reverse of boredom. [...] Exquisite sensibilities evoke the elementary furies of the beast. The Byronic hero, incapable of love, or only capable of an impossible love, suffers from 'spleen.' He is solitary, languid, his condition exhausts him. If he wants to feel alive, it must be in the terrible exaltation of a brief and destructive action." "The dandy creates his own unity by aesthetic means. But it is an aesthetic of singularity and of negation. 'To live and die before a mirror': that, according to Baudelaire, was the dandy's slogan. It is indeed a coherent slogan. The dandy is, by occupation, always in opposition. He can only exist by defiance. [...] He can only be sure of his own existence by finding it in the expression of others' faces. Other people are his mirror. A mirror that quickly becomes clouded, it is true, since human capacity for attention is limited. It must be ceaselessly stimulated, spurred on by provocation. The dandy, therefore, is always compelled to astonish." (180 and 182-83).

[192] With Ivan Karamazov, Fyodor Dostoevsky offers us "the tortured face of the rebel plunged in the abyss, incapable of action, torn between the idea of his own innocence and the desire to kill. He hates the death penalty because it is the image of the human condition, and, at the same time he is drawn to crime. Because he has taken the side of mankind, solitude is his lot. With him the rebellion of reason culminates in madness." (191).

tion" of the will to power (as in Stirner and Nietzsche[193]), finally to many different, often extreme forms of "revolt in poetry."[194]

This first *excursus* is followed by a second — on historical rebellion[195]. And then on "The Regicides,"[196] "The Deicides,"[197] "Individual Terrorism"[198], "State Terrorism and Irrational Terror,"[199] "State Terrorism and Rational Terror," State Terrorism and Irrational Terror"[200] and "Rebellion and Revolution." Finally, there is a third section

---

[193] "Advocate of classic taste, of irony, of frugal defiance, aristocrat who had the courage to say that aristocracy consisted of practicing virtue without asking for a reason [...], addict of integrity [...], stubborn supporter of the 'supreme equity of the supreme intelligence that is the mortal enemy of fanaticism,' he was set up, thirty-three years after his death, by his own countrymen as the master of lies and violence, and his ideas and virtues, made admirable by his sacrifice, have been rendered detestable [...]; we shall never finish making reparation for the injustice done to him." (207).

[194] "Rebel poetry, at the end of the nineteenth and the beginning of the twentieth century, constantly oscillated between these two extremes: between literature and the will to power, between the irrational and the rational, the desperate dream and ruthless action." (212).

[195] "History without a value to transfigure it, - writes Camus later on (416-17) - is controlled by the law of expediency. Historical materialism, determinism, violence, negation of every form of freedom which does not coincide with expediency and the world of courage and of silence, are the highly legitimate consequences of a pure philosophy of history."

[196] "Saint-Just, it seems, was responsible for Louis XVI's death; but when he exclaims: 'To determine the principle in virtue of which the accused is to die, is to determine the principle by which the society that judges him lives,' he demonstrates that it is the philosophers who are going to kill the King: the King must die in the name of the social contract" — even if "Rousseau would not, of course, have wanted this." (245).

[197] "The revolutionaries of the twentieth century have borrowed from Hegel the weapons with which they definitively destroyed the formal principles of virtue. All that they have preserved is the vision of a history without any kind of transcendence, dedicated to perpetual strife and to the struggle of will bent on seizing power. In its critical aspect, the revolutionary movement of our times is primarily a violent denunciation of the formal hypocrisy that presides over bourgeois society." "The entire history of mankind is in any case nothing but a prolonged fight to the death for the conquest of universal prestige and absolute power. It is in essence imperialist" (266 and 270).

[198] "In a universe of total negation, these young disciples try, with bombs and revolvers and also with the courage they show when they walk to the gallows, to [...] create the values they lack. Until their time, men died for what they knew, or for what they thought they knew. Since their time, this developed into the rather more difficult habit of sacrificing oneself for something about which one knew nothing, except that it was necessary to die so that it might exist. Until then, those who had to die put themselves in the hand of God in defiance of the justice of man. But reading the declarations of the condemned victims of that period [1878-1905], we are amazed to see that all, without exception entrusted themselves, in defiance of their judges, to the justice of other men who were not yet born." (297-98).

[199] Appealing to Hegel and Nietzsche (respectively), Mussolini and Hitler "illustrate, historically, some of the prophecies of German ideology. In this respect they belong to the history of rebellion and of nihilism. They were the first to construct a State on the concept that everything is meaningless, and that history is only a product of chance and force. The consequences were not long in appearing." (309).

[200] "Since Marx's death, in any case, only a minority of his disciples have remained faithful to

on rebellion and art[201]: "Rebellion and the Novel," "Rebellion and Style," and "Creation and Revolution."

It is an ample overview that, from its inception, focuses on the "rebirth" of rebellion as opposed to its degeneration. "Rebellion, in man, is the refusal to be treated as an object [...] It is the affirmation of a nature common to all men, which eludes the world of power" (381 and 382).

"Every great reformer tries to create in history what Shakespeare, Cervantes, Molière, and Tolstoy knew how to create: a world always ready to satisfy the hunger for freedom and dignity which every man carries in his heart. Beauty, no doubt, does not make revolutions. But a day will come when revolutions have need of beauty. [...] Is it possible eternally to reject injustice without ceasing to acclaim the nature of man and the beauty of the world? Our answer is yes. This ethic, at once unsubmissive and loyal, is in any event the only one that lights the way to a truly realistic revolution. In upholding beauty, we prepare the way for the day of regeneration when civilization will give first place [...] to this living virtue on which is founded the common dignity of man and the world he lives in, and which we must now define in the face of a world that insults it" (408).

5 — So the danger, always recurring in different forms, is that the rebel's legitimate intentions (and aspirations) will be overturned and betrayed. This is a key theme of *The Rebel* — a turbulent book, a raging

---

his method. The Marxists who have made history have, on the contrary, appropriated the prophecy and the apocalyptic aspects of his doctrine in order to realize a Marxist revolution, in the exact circumstances under which Marx had foreseen that a revolution could not take place." "The authoritarian socialists deemed that history was going too slowly and that it was necessary, in order to hurry it on, to entrust the mission of the proletariat to a handful of doctrinaires. For that very reason they have been the first to deny this mission. Nevertheless, it exists [...]. In order for it to manifest itself, however, a risk must be taken and confidence placed in working-class freedom and spontaneity. Authoritarian socialism, on the contrary, has confiscated this living freedom for the benefit of an ideal freedom, which is yet to arrive. In so doing, whether it wished to or not, it reinforced the attempt at enslavement begun by industrial capitalism. By the combined action of these two factors and over a hundred and fifty years, except in the Paris of the Commune, which was the last refuge of rebel revolution, the proletariat has had no other historical mission but to be betrayed." (Ibid. 318 and 349-50).

[201] "Van Gogh's admirable complaint is the arrogant and desperate cry of all artists. 'I can very well, in life and in painting, too, do without God. But I cannot, suffering as I do, do without something that is greater than I am, that is my life — the power to create.' [...] No form of art can survive on total denial alone. [...] Man can allow himself to denounce the total injustice that he alone will create. But he cannot affirm the total hideousness of the world. To create beauty, he must simultaneously reject reality and exalt certain of its aspects. Art disputes reality but does not hide from it." (389-90).

river that finally flows into a final chapter, "Thought at the Meridian" (in turn subdivided into three sections: "Rebellion and Murder," "Moderation and Excess," and "Beyond Nihilism").

The purpose of "solar" thinking, Camus explains, is to reject injustice while saluting the nature of man and the beauty of the world. "Far from this source of life, however, Europe and the revolution are being shaken to the core by a spectacular convulsion. [...] At the climax of contemporary tragedy, we therefore become intimates of crime. The sources of life and of creation seem exhausted. Fear paralyzes a Europe peopled with phantoms and machines. Between two holocausts, scaffolds are installed in underground caverns where humanist executioners celebrate their new cult in silence" (409).

This expresses the 'tragic feeling' of the author's life in the years of McCarthyism, Stalinism, and the onset of the Cold War. The argument inevitably turns to the left.

"The rebels who, united against death, wanted to construct a savage immortality on the foundation of the human species, are terrified at the prospect of being obliged to kill in their turn. Nevertheless, if they retreat, they must accept death; if they advance, they must accept murder. Rebellion, cutoff from its origins and cynically travestied, oscillates on all levels between sacrifice and murder. The form of justice that it advocated and that it hoped was impartial has turned out to be summary. [...] Must we therefore renounce every kind of rebellion, whether we accept, with all its injustices, a society that outlives its usefulness, or whether we decide, cynically, to serve, against the interest of man, the inexorable advance of history?" (410).[202]

The issue, obviously, is finding a new way. "But," Camus wonders, "are we still living in a rebellious world? Has not rebellion become, on the contrary, the excuse of a new variety of tyrant?" (lvi). These are questions which, by establishing lines of demarcation and calling to mind the extensive excursus mentioned above, undoubtedly enable the author to distinguish between genuine revolts and betrayed, manipulated uprisings.

"Logically, [...] murder and rebellion are contradictory." Nihilist murder claims total freedom, "the unlimited display of human pride."

---

[202] "After all," the passage continues, "if the logic of our reflection should lead to a cowardly conformism it would have to be accepted as certain families sometimes accept inevitable dishonor. If it must also justify all the varieties of attempts against man, and even his systematic destruction, it would be necessary to consent to this suicide. The desire for justice would finally realize its ambition: the disappearance of a world of tradesmen and police."

"Rebellion, on the contrary, puts total freedom on trial."[203] Historical murder is the consequence of historicist philosophy — "it wholeheartedly accepts the evil of history and in this way is opposed to rebellion." "If rebellion could find a philosophy, it would be a philosophy of limits, of calculated ignorance, and of risk" (418 and 419).[204]

6 — And so, we arrive at the heart of the matter — "moderation and excess." "The errors of contemporary revolution are first of all explained by the ignorance or systematic misconception of the limit which seems inseparable from human nature and which rebellion accurately reveals. [...] If the limit discovered by rebellion transfigures everything; if every thought, every action which goes beyond a certain point negates itself, there is in effect a measure by which to judge events and men. In history as in psychology, rebellion is an irregular pendulum which [...] moves around a pivot. While it suggests a nature common to all men, rebellion brings to light the measure and the limit which are the very principle of this nature" (Camus 1951; now 1962, iii, 423-24).

And so it happens that every reflection, material forces, the contradictions of thought in revolt, moral paradoxes, etc., reflect this law of proportion.

In the end, Camus argues, "at this limit the 'we are' defines a new form of individualism. [...] I need others who need me and each other. [...] I alone, in one sense, support the common dignity that I cannot allow either myself or others to debase. This individualism is in no sense pleasure, it is perpetual struggle and, sometimes, unparalleled joy when it reaches the heights of intrepid compassion" (426-27).

---

[203] "Every man, by that one act of revolt that rouses him to face the oppressor, thereby defends life, commits himself to struggle against servitude, lies and terror, and affirms, in a flash, that these three scourges enforce silence among men, obscure them from each other, and prevent them from rediscovering themselves in the only value that can save them from nihilism — the long complicity among men grappling with their destiny" (411,412 and 414).

[204] "Rational crime," Camus adds a bit further on (419-20, 420 and 422), "exercises itself, in the first place, on rebels whose insurrection contests a history which is henceforth deified. The mystification peculiar to the mind which claims to be revolutionary today sums up and increases bourgeois mystification." Rebellion "supposes a limit at which the community of man is established. Its universe is the universe of relative values. Instead of saying, with Hegel and Marx, that all is necessary, it only repeats that all is possible." "Does the end justify the means? That is possible. But what will justify the end? To that question, which historic thought leaves pending, rebellion replies — the means." (Which is to say, there is an identity between means and ends — as was argued, incidentally, by Eugenio Colorni [1931; now 2022, Ch.l] referring to the work of Machiavelli and Campanella).

"On the very day when the Caesarian revolution triumphed over the syndicalist and libertarian spirit, revolutionary thought lost, in itself, a counterweight that it cannot deprive itself of without decaying. This counterweight, this spirit which takes the measure of life, is the same that animates the long tradition of what can be called solar thinking, in which, from the Greeks onward, nature has always been poised for what is to come. The history of the First International, when German Socialism ceaselessly fought against the libertarian thought of the French, the Spanish, and the Italians, is the history of the struggle of German ideology against the Mediterranean mind. The commune against the State, concrete society against absolutist society, deliberate freedom against rational tyranny, finally altruistic individualism against the colonization of the masses, are then the contradictions that express once again the endless opposition of moderation to excess which has animated the history of the West since the time of the ancient world" (430).[205]

In fact, Camus adds (431), "historicist absolutism, despite its triumphs, has never ceased to come into collision with an irrepressible demand of human nature, of which the Mediterranean, where intelligence is intimately related to the blinding light of the sun, guards the secret. The conceptions faithful to the revolt, that of the Commune and that of revolutionary trade unionism, have not ceased to proclaim such demands in the face of both bourgeois nihilism and Caesarean absolutism."

III

7 — What can be said after so many years about a complicated, tangled text like *The Rebel*? First, it should be recalled that the book was not a success, even compared with Camus' other books. Harshly attacked from the left, it lost some of its topicality (and bite) with the death of Stalin. The author found himself isolated, his message unable to find traction in the political culture of the time.

And yet observed from the standpoint of "la pensée de midi," the book clearly contains numerous elements worthy of reflection —

---

[205] "Perhaps," the text continues (430-31), "the profound conflict of this century is [...] between German dreams and Mediterranean traditions, between the violence of eternal adolescence and virile strength, between nostalgia, rendered more acute by knowledge and by books and courage reinforced by the experience of life — in other words, between history and nature."

which perhaps can be re-proposed, *mutatis mutandis,* in other historical conditions and different frames of logic.

In the first place, the book puts at the center of the analysis the rebel faced with injustice (of any kind or degree) as the condition of his or her life. If they avoid the kinds of degeneration (nihilistic, historical-determinist, artistic, etc.) that might lead them to murder, Camus suggests, women and men can achieve significant results through rebellion — as in the case of revolutionary trade unionism, which "in one century, is responsible for the enormously improved condition of the workers from the sixteen-hour day to the forty-hour week" (429).

Moreover, in the wake of "Letters to a German Friend," *The Rebel* proposes an interpretive approach that is very different (in terms of theoretical 'slant' and period of reference) from the 'angles' we have seen in the first part of this work. It is not addressed to the Mediterranean, but rather to Europe as a whole (observed mainly from Paris) and to the last two centuries of revolt (that is, from the mid-eighteenth century onward) that shaped the political-social experience of the continent.

In fact, 'thought from the meridian' (or 'solar thinking') plays a key role in his argument only at the end of the book — in its advocacy of the 'proportion' essential to rebellion. But there are always traces of its influence in the fabric of the reasoning. Because it has always played a major role in European history and will doubtless continue to do so in the future.[206]

8 — At this point, while I was still groping in the dark, I caught sight, fortunately, of a providential coup de théâtre. In Paris, it is well known, as I have already mentioned, *L'homme révolté* was not successful. Less well known, on the other hand, is that Camus received strong support in this regard from French-Algerian culture, mainly due to Gabriel Audisio.[207]

I refer specifically to "Le génie de l'Afrique du Nord de Saint Agustin a Albert Camus"[208] which Audisio later took up in — "L'Algerien"

---

[206] "Authoritarian thought, by means of three wars [the Franco-Prussian war of 1870 and the two world wars] and thanks to the physical destruction of a revolutionary elite [the Paris Commune], has succeeded in submerging this libertarian tradition. But this barren victory is only provisional; the battle still continues. Europe has never been free of this struggle between darkness and light. It has only degraded itself by deserting the struggle and eclipsing day with night." (Ibid., 431).

[207] Inevitably, the observations that follow make no claim to being an assessment of Audisio's work in general, which I know only in part.

[208] Audisio 1954 — Text I received online courtesy of Dr. Miriam Begliuomini.

— his contribution to the special issue of *La nouvelle Revue Française* of March 1, 1960, "Hommage à Albert Camus 1913-1960" - dedicated precisely to the latter's tragic death. Indeed, from these short texts (perhaps accompanied by other readings) one can quickly learn some key additions that trace the elaboration of *L'homme révolté* back to the Mediterranean.

"The 'Centre Universitaire Mediterranéen'," Audisio said as he began "Le génie de l'Afrique du Nord" (Algiers Conference, Dec. 12, 1953) (Audisio 1954, 151), "asked me to speak to you about North Africa in a certain way; that is, to search through the centuries and in contemporary times for what may constitute the essence of its genius, as manifested in the men most qualified to express it. Namely, in thinkers, philosophers, writers."

And in "L'Algerien" — the 1960 tribute to Camus — we read that after trying to understand Camus' influence on contemporary Berber, Arab and Jewish literati, as well as on those of European descent born and educated in North Africa, Audisio came to the conclusion that Algeria "is a 'torrential' country, where immoderation reigns in the physical climate as in the spirits, provoking in men, or at least in the best of them, a constant effort to master themselves and the elements. Tertullian, who was himself an example of this, was already aware of it... This is a long tradition that is likely to impose itself on Algerian writers, even when they are not aware of it. I happened to reflect on it and talk about it often"-to the point that when Camus published *L'homme révolté*, Audisio exclaimed in his Algiers Conference, "I suddenly said to myself, 'isn't it, by any chance, that Camus would have rebelled in the first place because he is African?'" (Audisio 1960, 435; 1954, 152).

This is, of course, a joke (une boutade) that nonetheless emphasizes "the very violent contrasts, the extreme diversity, the disparities, which are pushed to the point of contradiction by the North African nature". It is an observation that, if I am not mistaken, helps to understand, conversely, the key role that the theme of measurement plays in the writing of *L'homme révolté* and the Mediterranean libertarian influence that this issue has had on European thought on several occasions.

9 — This then gives rise to a second, important aspect of the whole issue. Along with his Algerian origins, Audisio generalizes the problematic of *L'homme révolté* to North African history in general and thus

to twenty centuries and more — centuries of extremes and revolts.[209] "However far one goes back in time," he stated, "one sees, this North Africa, constantly characterized by a dualism, by a conflict between two extremes, or between different extremes" (156): between East and West, between nomadic and sedentary peoples, between monotheism and polytheism, between superstition and religion, between reality and the supernatural, between paradisiacal and asceticism, between impurity and sanctity, between spirit and instinct, between civilizations-the dominant ones that followed one another-and barbarism (or rather "berberies" in the sense of Berber, indigenous[210]).

At the same time, multiple forms of rebellion have emerged in North Africa. "The is that courage and the spirit of resistance go hand in hand, they walk together. Throughout centuries, North Africans have been subjected to foreign domination. They have always resisted, and insurrections have always occurred among them. They were perpetual insurrections, and I would say almost [...] that one saw among them 'l'homme révolté' of which Camus speaks, in an almost perpetual way. Certainly, it is not fortuitously that Camus attaches so much importance and so much attention to the revolt" (156).

But, if these North Africans," Audisio (159) continued, "constantly seek each other between these extremes, they must inevitably, at certain moments, pass through a point that can be called a point of equilibrium, and they are likely to try to reach that point on which to stop. [...] Intellectually, in thought, this must be represented by attempts at intellectual synthesis. Well, for my part [...] I have seen them produce, I think, at least three times those attempts. There is a great synthesis that was made in ancient times, that of St. Augustine; there is a second one that was made in Muslim times: it is that of Ibn Khaldûn"; as for the third, we shall see, it could occur before our eyes: it would be that of Albert Camus.

"There is no doubt," Audisio clarified, "that in ancient times, in Roman times, the greatest of Africans, Augustine, was certainly the first to find, after having passionately sought it, this sense of the measure he

---

[209] More precisely, he applies to the specifics of North African history, the logic that Camus tends to generalize from the two centuries of European history under consideration; see, above, sec. 6 of this chapter.
[210] This is, if I am not mistaken, the rationale for Audisio's numerous self-deprecating mentions of his "barbarism" that we encountered above (cfr. Ch. 1, sec 13 and n. 112 Ch. 2). In other words: he manifests in that way his need to keep himself connected to the "Berber" populations, indigenous.

needed, knowing all too well the immensity that was in him. You know as well as I do that, he fought on all fronts in the Church to arrive finally at that great intellectual construction that is the City of God. And he built this great construction of the spirit, solid and lasting for centuries, at the very moment when the Roman Empire was collapsing, at the very moment when the Goths were in Rome, while he himself died in his villa in Hippo, our Bona of today, which was besieged by the Vandals. Well, he was leaving at that moment there the most enduring thought, certainly the most classical thought of the age."

"The same phenomenon," continued Audisio, "occurred in the Muslim era. Toward the end of our Middle Ages, at a time when infighting and the disintegration of governments and institutions reigned in the Maghreb, Ibn Khaldûn, who took refuge for many years in a kind of casbah, a remote castle on the Frenda side of the Onanese, drafted the *Prolegomenon* of his great history, which is certainly the synthesis of the North African spirit of that era. It is a work of an extraordinary boldness of thought for the time, since it could frequently and rightly be written that the author in some way revealed himself in it as a forerunner of a Montesquieu or an Auguste Compte. And he too is a classic and, like the Latins, he too is a moralist."

10 — Personally, before tackling the reading to the third synthesis, which, as we shall see was (could not be, is) by no means concluded, I would have liked to know more about the first two - out of sheer curiosity and to place them better in my inherited culture (which, as I wrote at the beginning, is in urgent need of restoration). For example, I would have liked to read Augustine in depth and understand how his thought later influenced other parts of the Roman Empire - such as Southern Italy, which was also burdened, as is well known, by successive dominations. And perhaps I would have liked to realize whether and how (to refer to Semitic philosophical thought) the Islamic Averroes and the Jewish Maimonides of Cordova influenced the formation of the historian and essayist Ibn Khaldûn whose *Prolegomenon*, (i.e., his "Introduction to History, the classical Islamic history of the world") suddenly opens to knowledge an extraordinary collective horizon of which we have hitherto been culpably ignorant.

But the desire to get to the point quickly prevailed in me (and to postpone curiosity and further study until a later date). "There is no doubt," Audisio said again in his December 1953 lecture (160), "that all Algerian writers, who, as you know, are at present very numerous, have for the most part in common this tendency toward classicism." I think, on the other hand, that "one could amuse oneself by finding expressions of classical style in Camus's writing, linking him back to his Latin precursors. I believe that there are in Camus some traits of style that are very close to those of Augustine's writing. [...] This tendency toward classicism is the search that North Africans make for measure, because they know the disproportion that is in them [...]. Camus knows this so well that after talking so long about revolt, what does he land on? He lands - these are his words - to a 'solar thought,' to a 'pensée de midi,' to what Valery already called 'midi le juste'; he lands to the thought of a character who is dear to me in more than a particular way, to Ulysses[211] [...]. And what did this Ulysses seek? He was looking for the conditions of an ordinary man, that is, the narrow measure of the man who rejects all temptations of excess [...]. Wary of what is torrential in their climate and spirit, the North Africans come to correct its foreseeable effects by voluntary discipline, just as their engineers regulate waterways."

We have thus come to the point. After the Algerian War, which has been under the radar since 1944, then exploded between 1954 and 1962, and was painfully experienced; and after all that has happened thereafter (autocracies, terrorisms, Arab Springs, etc.) and is still happening up to us, shouldn't we at least speak conditionally, in the sense that the North Africans could, should also correct their inequities?

And if one argues with Audisius that Augustine, Ibn Khaldûn, and their emulators were committed writers (engages) for the public good, should one not point again to solutions of that kind?

And if so, after the first pre-war phase of 'la pensée de midi" and after the post-war phase animated again, but with reversed parts, by Camus and Audisio, should not a third one be fostered, capable of involving first-hand new committed intellectuals of Berber and Arab origin?[212]

---

[211] Audisio alludes here, evidently to his *Usysse ou l'intelligence*, 1946.
[212] These are questions that do not, however, prevent us from identifying in the present (with Audisio 1954, 161) "a direction toward the future, that sort of constant among Africans that is humanism." If nothing else, Plautus wrote a work called The Carthaginians. Terence, according to whom "nothing that is human is foreign to me," was born in Carthage. St. Augustine's humanism, you know him." Ibn Khaldûn "is the father of what one might call Muslim humanism, Islamic humanism. He has words that go a long way with respect to his belief in the

11 -On the other hand, the need to refer to "la pensée de midi" in order to move forward in Europe beyond nihilism and beyond Hegelian-Marxist historicism inevitably poses a problem that is not explicitly spelled out in the text — that of the relationship between European and Mediterranean thinking. In the sense that at this point one must ask — if the latter has always played a key role in reforming the former, what has happened and will happen to the inverse relation between them?

That is to say, by gradually generalizing this 'Camusian discovery,' could we not develop the idea of a possible interaction (fruitful or not) between northern and southern Europe, between Europe and the Mediterranean[213], between Europe and Africa, between the north and south of the planet?[214]

Also, this question inevitably assumes even greater importance when we think (with the benefit of hindsight) about the parallel lives of Gabriel Audisio and Albert Camus, on one hand, and Eugenio Colorni and Albert Hirschman, on the other.[215]

Neighbors (without knowing it) in respective rebellions of the mid-1930s, they then embarked on different paths. Camus took that of militant journalism and publishing, Colorni of socialist Europeanist federalism and the Resistance, Audisio of anti-fascist governmental public service and of the study "le génie de la Méditerranée," and Hirschman of exile in the United States (after having accomplished an extraordinary exploit in Marseilles with Varian Fry).

Nevertheless, in the case of all four of these protagonists, the Mediterranean experience made itself felt in the pursuit of their respective activities. Camus, forced to abandon Algiers, would write for metro-

---

goodness of man, in original humanism. [...] There is always in North Africans this kind of feeling of human fraternity that was indicated very well by Amrouche: 'we are people, he said, who naturally call each other brothers.' And it's true."

[213] Of course, also to make concrete the hope (or perhaps vaticinium) manifested by Audisio in concluding his Algiers Conference. "I believe," he said (ibid. 162), "to conclude, that the North African man has recently become aware of himself as such, as a North African man, but that, for all that is happening today, it is as if the hour of this awareness has actually arrived. So the hope that we must formulate, and that I, who have lived close to these men for a long time, who have studied and practiced them so much, the hope that I formulate is that the spirit of revolt and secession that has always been in their 'genius' [...] will not distract them from the fraternal humanism that I am talking to you about and that is also in their 'genius'."

[214] And further, by analogy, between Western Europe and Central-Eastern Europe (now under attack by the Russian Federation), and more generally between East and West.

[215] This is mentioned above (in sec. 2 of Ch. 1). The first in each pair — I would add — is older than the latter (Audisio much older than Camus and Colorni older than Hirschman), while they differ as to political temperament (Camus and Colorni are more militant) and professional success (greater in Camus and Hirschman).

politan France. The further 'southernization' of Colorni — at Ventotene and Melfi — would play an important part in his political choices and his ultimate sacrifice (while Altiero Spinelli, Ernesto Rossi and Ursula Hirschmann led the battle for a united Europe). Finally, Albert Hirschman would work on the Marshall Plan (and then in Colombia).

In other words, in the process of change that came about with the world war, our 'dramatis personae' felt, each in his own way, the need for theoretical-practical interaction between traditionally separate areas of the world, carrying north options that initially arose in the south (i.e., representing an *ante litteram* "south wind"[216]), and, perhaps unintentionally, opening the path that we are especially interested in here — that of dynamic imbalance-rebalance and interaction.

This is why, as soon as I had the opportunity to compare them,[217] the 'Camusian' experience in Algiers and Colorni's in Trieste in the 1930s struck me as crucial and innovative, even at such a remove in time. They even appeared as two sides of the same expected future coin, which we will have to grapple with (beginning in the pages that follow) if we are to keep faith with a libertarian (and liberating) orientation in a world in turmoil.

"European Pride, Mediterranean Pride" — the aim of the present work is to start plumbing this issue, prioritizing the Mediterranean (and not, as usual, Europe — like it or not) but with an eye on the practicalities of the present.

12 — There is "a thought," Camus remarks in 1951 at tire close of *The Rebel*, "which the world today cannot do without for very much longer. There is, undoubtedly, in the Russian people something to inspire Europe with the potency of sacrifice, and in America a necessary constructive power. But the youth of the world always find themselves standing on the same shore. Thrown into the unworthy melting-pot of Europe, deprived of beauty and friendship, we Mediterraneans, the proudest of

---

[216] These are, as I have already mentioned, two different points of view - one (more) literary, the other (more) scientific - that can complement each other, since the former has a very attractive Mediterranean evocative role, while the latter allows for a more theoretical-practical understanding of the situation. Moreover, they solidly have a "neutral" attitude (and thus also a vocation of companions, of "bridges") towards the two major mass religiosities prevailing on the two shores of the Mediterranean. Yet, while moving in the opposite direction - from south to north and north to south - they are inevitably part of the Western culture (from whose bosom they sprang) and would need to interrelate with similar but different (especially Eastern) points of view in order to progress further.

[217] Cf. sec. 2 of Ch. 1 and the previous note.

races, live always by the same light. In the depths of the European night, solar thought, the civilization facing two ways, awaits its dawn."[218] Thus, the argument of this remarkable book returns at the end to "la pensée de midi." The reader will recall that at the beginning of *Jeunesse* Audisio spoke of the eternal Mediterranean, but then, during the course of his argument, he repeatedly returned to the vibrant daily life of this part of the world.[219] Here Camus seems instead to follow an opposite procedure, focusing his attention on the last two centuries of European rebellion in reference to the youthfulness of the world, which the Mediterranean has always managed to renew.

This may take the reader's curiosity back to origins. And this would justify (even *post factum*) the brief exploration of the history and proto history of the central Mediterranean which, while drawing on Audisio's work on Carthage, I reviewed above, in the second and third chapters of this volume.

So what was it I was looking for — I asked myself — in that age of city-states (both home-grown and imported) in our part of the world, and in the historical process that in the end drove so many peoples into the capacious arms of the national-imperialism we know so well — that 'shirt of Nessus' that has been historically repeated a hundred times in new forms and which (then and now) has never ceased to torment us?[220] I clearly wished to convince myself that another way of life might nevertheless have been possible, and perhaps that still *another way might exist in the future* if we were only capable of going against the trend. Of moving, that is, from the national-imperialist era in which we find ourselves (and have for more than two millennia!) toward a democratic federalism tending to be libertarian, egalitarian, solidarity-based, fraternal, and effectively triumphant on an ever larger, planetary scale.

It is this daydream which, starting with the progressive empowerment and civilizing of Cattanean memory, Eugenio Colorni proposed as a goal for European unity and as a point of transition to world federalism.

---

[218] Camus 1951; now 1962, iii, 432. Two references may be noted in this passage — one to Audisio's *Jeunesse*, and the other to the civilization with a double face, European and African... or even past and future.
[219] Cf., for example, n. 50 of Ch. 1.
[220] By this, I certainly do not mean to deny the complexity and tortuousness of human history, its successes and misfortunes, nor the many lessons that can be learned from it. I only wish to note that, despite the vast amount of water that has passed under the bridge, humankind has not yet managed to work out a solution to this basic issue of force, power, domination and thus subordination, which has continually resurfaced historically in new forms.

My question: could *la jeunesse mediterranéenne* and measured Camusian revolt "work" as clean energy — as a starting engine for this welcome adventure to be set in motion again starting from (and involving) the Mediterranean?

Might not such a prospect in itself represent an attractive objective in renewing the youth of the Mediterranean and allowing it to join with that of others? Would it not also represent a powerful antidote to the impoverishment of our lives, 'against the wear and tear of modern life' to speak euphemistically,[221] against loss of meaning — ennui, melancholy, depression destructive nihilism, Hegelian historicism, stress?

It is this Mediterranean pride (past, present, and future) that I would finally like to explore with a few transitory strokes of the pen, discussing along the way the possible means to be used, so as to adapt them to the goal.

---

[221] To borrow (with a hint of self-irony) a famous advertisement from my youth.

CHAPTER 5

"Get what I'm saying?"[222]

In 2020, Wolf Lepenies, ex-'assistant' of Albert Hirschman and Clifford Geertz during the now-legendary 'Interpretive Social Science' period at the Institute for Advanced Study at Princeton, published a volume for the "Maison des sciences de l'homme" in Paris entitled *Le pouvoir en Méditerranée. Un rêve français pour una autre Europe*. In the foreword to this edition [223] he presented the subject of the book, the history of the long-standing 'dream' of French Mediterranean politics of "forming in Europe a coalition of the southern countries and thereby determining the fate of the continent" (Lepenies 2020,10).[224] In the "Acknowledgments" at the end of the book, Lepenies wrote: "Grâce à sa magnifique exposition 'Le Noir et le Bleu. Un rêve méditerranéen...' au Musée des civilisations de l'Europe et de la Méditerranée (MuCEM), puis en tant que membre de l'Institut d'études avancées de l'Université d'Aix-Marseille (IMéRA), Thierry Fabre m'a ouvert de nouvelles perspectives sur la Méditerranée."

Curious about this 'ending' (and of course in agreement with Nicoletta Stame), I decided to acquire the sumptuous catalog of the show which, under the patronage of an impressive number of institutions, artists, and Mediterranean and European cultural organizations, was held from 7 June 2013 to 6 January 2014 in Marseilles-Provence (then the European Capital of Culture). The observations that follow represent a (partial) synthesis of my impressions of it.

First of all, Thierry Fabre, its "Commissaire générale," authored the exhibition's captivating introduction. "Il y a comme une énigme," he writes, "dans cet alliage de couleurs. Le Noir et le Bleu... Goya et

---

[222] Rough translation of *"Capita came?"* an ironic (and self-deprecating) dialectal catchphrase, typically Tarquinese.
[223] The original German edition was published by C.H. Verlag in Munich in 2016.
[224] "Nurturing an 'ambition for the Mediterranean,' explains the back cover, has been an essential component of French policy since the end of the Napoleonic empire. This policy, which aims to form a coalition among the different peoples of the 'privileged sea' (as Fernand Braudel called it), is proposed as a counterweight to Germany's influence on Europe. For this reason, as a way of standing up to the Slavic and Germanic empires, many generations of [French] policymakers considered the formation of a 'Latin Bloc,' a 'Mediterranean Union,' or even, giving it a particularly aggressive and significant title, a 'Latin Empire.'"

Miro." The evil reality and the dream of good. It was immediately clear that the exhibition's center of gravity would be positioned first and foremost on the artistic-literary side of the Mediterranean equation — where Lepenies's evaluation *(magnifique)* appeared at first glance to be fully justified.

Nevertheless, I said to myself, this need not prevent the extensive, elegant material collected here from being observed from other points of view as well, such as the 'Mediterranean perspectives' of particular interest to me. In any case, 'no harm in trying.' I started flipping through this big book of nearly four hundred pages full of illustrations, paintings, and period photos, divided into twelve 'moments' (and accompanied by a rich glossary).

The presentation of the second 'moment,' "Conquest and Civilization," made me stop and think. "In the 19th century," I read (AA.VV. 2013, 39), "the Europeans thought that civilization, an idea that arose during the Enlightenment, was not *a* civilization but THE civilization. The word civilization was then contrasted with nature and then also with *barbarism*. This gave the Europeans a justification for their conquests: the expedition to Egypt [of Napoleon Bonaparte] was designed to spread the Enlightenment for the purpose of rebuilding society and the society of Algiers [of Charles X] wanted to leave the land of barbarism. While scientific explorations were being conducted under the protection of gunfire, the conquest was being conducted in the name of a "civilizing mission."

Are we so sure, my French friends — it occurred to me at this point — that we have left this way of thinking behind for good? If so, then why would French rulers have cultivated the goal of dominating the Mediterranean for so long (as Lepenies has thoroughly documented)?[225] And furthermore — if we have, then what would account for the sense of unreasonable, snobbish superiority displayed openly by so many fellow citizens (French and Italian) instinctively even within our respective countries?

To understand this better, I turned my attention at this point to the eighth 'moment,' "A Broken and Reinvented Dream." From Smyrna in 1922 to Algiers in 1962, it maintains (AA.VV. 2013, 141), through "civil wars, the desire to regain sovereignty, the expulsion and deportation of peoples, the violence of history ripped through the entire Mediterranean. [...] But the Mediterranean dream [would] soon be reinvented

---

[225] Cf. above, n. 224.

after the war by the world of knowledge as well as the world of art and poetry."

From this — in the twelfth 'moment,' a small 'glorious' conclusion finally springs forth, "A Salvo for the Future..." (236). The response "in the face of [...] hatred and fear is 'the love of differences' that Michelangelo Pistoletto builds up as a symbol in his mirror table of the Mediterranean. The horizon opens with the upheaval of the Arab revolution in Tunis, Cairo and Tripoli, like the protests of the people in the public squares in Madrid or Athens. The nightmare of violence, obscurantism and hatred are never far away, but a dream, that never ceases to return, is being fulfilled before our eyes."

I

1 — What to say? I wish! I wish that had been the case. I wish it were true. Frankly... I'm just not convinced by this conclusion.[226] I certainly have no desire to underestimate the importance of the "stubborn dream," or the "foolish dreamer," and I would not cast doubt on the utility of a dialogue with artists and writers, or the many protagonists of the Mediterranean scene (with whom, for historical reasons, our French friends are far more familiar than we Italians). Nor (God forbid!) would I dispute the "right to dream" of Muslim leaders, many of whom, from a variety of eras, are rightly featured in this exhibition.

I just think that "dreams" and "salvos" aimed at the future, useful as they are (and unfortunately often denied by the actual course of historical reality), are not enough. They tend, if anything, to reproduce themselves indefinitely — unless they are backed up (this is my hypothesis) by conscious will and behavior, both individual and collective, addressed to the concrete situation, and possibly coming from the most diverse sectors of society.

To explain myself — without in any way detracting from the literary-artistic role of the question; indeed, with a conscious desire to support its momentum — let me briefly summarize my research.[227]

I shall begin with Gabriel Audisio's "Mediterranean Homeland,"

---

[226] Just think of what happened only a few years later to the "Arab Spring" that had raised the hopes of so many, or the "protests of the people in the public squares," who abandoned the field to... new "occupants." Should we not question the importance (and limits) of what happened?

[227] And in so doing to take a step backwards, to Chap. 1, Thierry Fabre's *Eloge de la pensée de midi* and the need to relate reasoning to practice; as, indeed, I argued in the introduction to Meldolesi, ed., 2022.

the eternal Mediterranean (perhaps 'deep'[228] is the better word) and its reassuring permanence, [229] able to transform and (up to a point) absorb the pressures from the outside, and to renew itself and re-emerge.[230] I continue with the "love of differences" that evolve over time and that energize the Mediterranean (the "inland sea," Fernand Braudel called it). I note that one of these has a very long history of confrontation, right from the time of the formation of the Mediterranean languages (which branched, it has been traditionally argued, from Indo-Persian and Semitic trunks). But even in the light of recent Islamic terrorism it remains important to promote what unites rather than divides us, and that for this purpose every actor can usefully play his or her part, in the myriad dimensions of life.[231]

2 — It is clear, moreover, that in the face of the many Mediterranean ups and downs, we need not lose heart. I understand the moments of discouragement, even in the trailblazers as Nietzsche and Camus undoubtedly were, in different eras. But reacting is essential. The purpose of this last chapter is not least to cast doubt on a somewhat despairing Nietzschean statement by Albert Camus — "there remains only history and power." [232] Fortunately, this may not be the case.

---

[228] Deeper than the civilizations to which it gave rise. (These, Braudel writes — 1987 103-04 — "move through time, triumphing over its duration. While the film of history is being made, they remain, imperturbable, in their place. In a sense, just as imperturbably, they remain masters of their own space, for the territory they occupy may vary at the margins, but at the core, in the central zone, their domain, their seat, they remain the same. [...] Such immobility means that civilizations sink into a past that is even more ancient, much more, than it seems at first glance, and long duration necessarily becomes part of their nature. Romanness does not begin with Christ. Islam does not begin with the seventh century, with Muhammad. And the Orthodox world does not begin with the founding of Constantinople in 330." Civilizations "survive metamorphoses and catastrophes and rise from their ashes when necessary. Destroyed, or at least damaged, they spring up again like crabgrass.")
[229] Cf. above, secs. 1,4, 7 and 8 of Ch. 1.
[230] The existence of such a "deposit" is obviously a cornerstone of the framing of "la pensée de midi," as it is of "our Mezzogiorno." But understandably (considering the respective formation of the two initiatives) the Franco-Algerian one has stressed the relevance of such a mine, while the southern one has focused on the policy consequences (positive and negative) that can be drawn from it. I hope that the present work will facilitate dialogue and integration between the two points of view.
[231] In this regard, the initiative of the "Rencontres Averroès" headed by Thierry Fabre, and more generally the many initiatives of this author involving Mediterranean intellectuals from all backgrounds is undoubtedly commendable. As for Italy, which, Braudel argued, "is more oriental than it would like you to believe," I think it could play a more proactive role in the future. While Israel, despite its well-known difficulties, is perhaps achieving a better Middle Eastern 'positioning,' with the recent Abraham Accords.
[232] In this passage history is intended as the powerful para-Hegelian current in its various

Our theme so far has taken on multiple guises that we can freely make use of: "Jeunesse de la Méditerranée," "New Mediterranean Culture," "The Rebel," "Thought from the Meridian," "Solar Thought." These titles are used at different times to denote multiple, often similar problems, observed from different spatio-temporal angles. They suggest 'jointly and severally' their current use in the *plural*, not the singular (just as Albert Hirschman would have advised). [233]

As I have already mentioned, the rebellious women and men studied in Camus's 'thinking at the meridian' in his 1951 essay lived in the two previous centuries. They are discussed by an author from the South, but are related to Europe proper and from Paris, from that powerful post-World War II "megaphone" (as Fernand Braudel called it). The multiple ramifications of these thoughts should be appreciated and preserved precisely because they refresh the soul like sea breezes. Because, as I quoted already, "the peoples born from the Mediterranean, burdened by centuries and civilizations, are always able to regenerate and sprout anew, like the laurel near a spring" (Audisio 1935, 52 and 53).

It thus happens that Southern thoughts can from time-to-time open particular dimensions that then suggest further developments characterized by different, carefully delimited analytical 'thrusts' and can even influence Northern thinking. [234]

3 — But as we know, at the end of 1954 the war in Algeria broke out. Inevitably, this event turned Mediterranean thinking on its head, [235]

---

representations (on the left and the right), and power is understood as the will and actual exercise of national and imperial power that inevitably involves the subordination of others — a key aspect of nationalism and imperialism that we all unfortunately know, and which continues to tower over us.

[233] I remember in particular that when it came to choosing the title of an anthology of his political essays that I edited, *Come far passare le riforme* 1990 *(How Reforms Should Be Passed,* 2021), Albert Hirschman insisted that *reforms* should be plural (rather than the singular *la riforma,* which would have been more normal in Italian and French).

[234] In this regard it seems to me that Camus's point of view represents a step forward even compared with Colorni's. Colorni was aware (obviously) of the marginal position of Italy (and the Roman Resistance in particular) with respect to what was happening (or what he thought might happen, but didn't) in the center of Europe, in Germany. He nevertheless thought that events in Rome would have some influence on the outcome of the war. Perhaps, reasoning in the manner of Camus, he could have 'said more.' That is, the southern wind initiated by the Four Days of Naples and activities to sabotage the enemy in the center of the country would have inspired, encouraged and matured similar ideas in northern Italy (and would even have played some role in making up for the tragic behavior of the German people at that juncture).

[235] I am referring, of course, to Jean Granier, Gabriel Audisio and Albert Camus, but also to other protagonists of the French colonial sphere, such as Jacques Berque (1998).

not least because it was based on the implicit assumption that it was possible, and in everyone's interests, to build peacefully on the coexistence, *sic et simpliciter,* of the different Mediterranean peoples. The war undermined this point of view and showed unapologetically that the world of the French settlers even those who had appreciated the culture and way of life of the Arabs and Berbers could not represent the dream of most of the Algerian population.

Albert Camus was saddened by this, but he reacted. In 1958 he brought together his writings on Algeria,[236] adding an extensive introduction that refused to come down on one side or the other 'of the barricade' and the tragic trail of violence that had ensued: the attacks, repression, massacres, torture, reprisals, napalm.

Of course, we can only hypothesize what Camus might have written about the last phase (and conclusion) of the Algeria war (since, as known, a tragic car accident suddenly deprived us of his genius).

But ultimately, however understandable on a personal level, his inability to 'take sides' has turned out in retrospect to be more important than it might seem. For it is tantamount to admitting that reasoning about "la pensée de midi" from before and after the war (and later), has often been conducted at a level of over-generalization that fails to take note of the 'vertical' relations of domination that exist in the Mediterranean (and thus of the need to soften them and then get rid of them perhaps gradually).

Such reasoning does not represent the hopes of most Mediterranean peoples. On the contrary despite the good intentions of their authors, they might even raise the suspicion that many such high-minded pro-Mediterranean pronouncements are carrying water to the usual mill. In other words, they actually conceal, even unintentionally, a pretense possibly only 'cultural' to traditional French hegemony.

---

[236] "Misère de la Kabylie" (1939), "Crise en Algérie" (1945), "Lettre a en militant algérien" (1955), "L'Algérie déchirée" (1956), "Appel pour une trêve civil" (1956), "L'affaire Maisonseul" (1956), "Algérie" (1958) [Camus 1958; 1962, iv, 253 and ff.]. "This volume," the author added at the last minute. (1958, 7), "had already been set in type and was about to appear when the events of May 13 occurred [the coup d'état of general Massu at Algiers]. After giving some thought to the matter, I decided that it was still worth publishing; indeed, that it was in a way a direct commentary on these events, and that given the current confusion, the positions and possible solutions set forth here deserved more than ever to be heard." Camus ultimately concluded from these that "the only acceptable future," which, however, would prove to be a mere wish (and regrettably unrealistic), was one "in which France, wholeheartedly embracing its tradition of liberty, does justice to all the communities of Algeria without discrimination in favor of one or another."

II

4 — How then do we break out of this impasse, at what is now a considerable distance from decolonization and the Cold War? How to fit into what Clifford Geertz has called "a world in pieces," which today, however, after the tragic invasion of Ukraine, seems to be in the process of reassembling itself? How do we set about 'mending it,' this world of ours, European and Mediterranean, even at the micro level?[237]

My advice would be first of all to test Camus's ideas with his own way of thinking.[238] And this would mean bringing his line of reasoning back, not least methodologically, to its human 'measure,' gradually reducing its level of generalization.

For example: explicitly recognize the existence of extra- and inter-Mediterranean vertical relationships; accentuate the provisional aspect of the reasoning developed so far; recognize their territorial (cultural, linguistic, social, etc.) origin; compare and rework them in the light of others' contributions; and at the same time explore at a lower level of generalization (middle range) the order of the issues they have raised (more or less explicitly).

I would like to concentrate on this last point. From the outset, the intention of the present work has been to take out of mutual isolation[239] (and at the same time anchor 'on the ground') the relevant traditions of intellectual thought that have emerged in the Mediterranean — from the Audisio-Camus to the Colorni-Hirschman tradition, and to others that may possibly be considered at a later date. To assess their compatibility, integrability, and practical applicability. So that their revival, evolution and possible (expected future) contribution can be properly evaluated. And, indeed, a reasoned exemplification of this particular perspective is where I would like finally to begin the concluding argument, which necessarily reflects mine and my collaborators' experience over the past four decades.

---

[237] Cf. Geertz 1999, Meldolesi 2016, Ch. 2 e 3.
[238] Cf. above, Ch. 4, sec. 6.
[239] Paraphrasing Leibniz, one might say that the differing theoretical-practical Mediterranean experiences are at the same time part of the same family, but continually risk inadvertently closing themselves off in "monadic" mutual isolation (whether local, regional, or national).

5 — Let us place ourselves in our minds[240] in the Mezzogiorno and ask ourselves (from a vantage point built up over eons) what we can set in motion to get ourselves started (intellectually, practically) on the intended path toward the development of solar, southern thinking[241] (instead of merely 'dreaming,' 'hoping for the best,' or acceding, perhaps with arms spread, to some form of historical determinism). The answer can be formulated in successive steps[242] such that, like tiles in a mosaic under construction, numerous aspects encountered earlier now mysteriously find their reasonable place in a discourse that nevertheless remains 'open.'

Step one ('the setting,' we can call it).

We need to take account of the general situation we find ourselves in (global, European, Mediterranean, local). For this purpose, we may look to Eugenio Colorni's 'lesson'[243] of May-July 1943 when he wrote to Altiero Spinelli explaining that contrary to what the two of them had initially assumed at Ventotene, a united Europe would not emerge spontaneously from Germany's defeat as a kind of trick of Hegelian-historical logic — that is, through the (unintended) effect of the 'eradication' of the old ruling classes by Hitler.

And in addition, the victorious great powers would not behave at all the way they did after the World War I, refraining from intervention in the internal affairs of the defeated countries (far from it!). Whereas, on the other hand, an eventual German revolution (which did not occur) could lead to a merger with the Soviet Union and thus trigger a new war.[244]

---

[240] This caveat is necessary because — to continue in the Leibnizian vein of the previous note — the different placement is a key aspect in the immense differentiation of monads (i.e., the enormous diversity, portrayed by Michelangelo Pistoletto in "Le Noir et le Bleu" — see above, the beginning of this chapter).

[241] It is thus clear that the procedure is now the reverse of the one just mentioned. In fact, whereas before it was a matter of reducing top-down generalization, now — through an exemplification that elevates a long-established social practice — the level of generalization increases, precisely so as to proceed to an intermediate, mutually comprehensible level applicable to other concrete situations.

[242] Fueled, as the reader will understand on the fly, by doubt along with mental mobility — curious, perceptive, and constantly effervescent.

[243] Colorni 2019a, iii, Ch. 3 and 4.

[244] "A Russo-German bloc set on the conquest of Europe would in all probability bring about a third world war (but, I hasten to add, it would truly be a definitive war for European unity [...]. In the Italian Risorgimento there were three wars. And I am not at all sure that to best implement and complete European unity a third war may not be necessary [...])" (Colorni 2019a, 163-64).

Alternatively, Eugenio argued, European unity might develop by degrees from within the divided world that emerged at the end of World War II, as a result of the influence that various peoples would be able to exert on the political swings of the victorious powers.[245]

"The two winning states, each the arbiter of a piece of our continent," Colorni wrote (Colorni 2019a, 160), "have two paths open to them. One is a policy of housekeeping, of internal reconstruction, reinforcing the ruling class, repaying their own people for their sacrifices during the war by improving their economic conditions and promoting their psychological position as 'winners' [...]. Or, there is the other path — joining with the vanquished, constituting with them a true and deeply-rooted unity; absorbing their lifeblood and civilizing forces; reconstructing together, sharing power with their ruling classes and letting them participate in leading the new unity being created; and facing the other half of Europe as a compact, aggressive bloc, endowed with an immensely strong power of popular attraction."

Clearly, it is this second solution that ended up prevailing for many years in the West. But then the situation changed. The United States changed its policy, tilting in favor of the first solution — which unquestionably changed the game (and forced new situations onto the rest of the world that it was not — we were not — prepared for).[246] And the political-military vacuum thus created facilitated the emergence of the very serious current crisis triggered by the Russian invasion of Ukraine.

The result is that having learned from Colorni and Hirschman the art of possibilist conjecture, we ourselves must incrementally delineate (and monitor and never lose sight of) the worldwide, Western, European and Mediterranean *setting* in which we move.

Step two ('stabilization and initiative').

The terrorist turn of 2001 (mentioned above, in Ch. 2) ushered in an era of further US expansionism followed by retreat, which, by promoting and then discouraging numerous social movements for freedom

---

[245] And in addition, Colorni argued, given Europe's (economic-political-cultural) location, its union could be a decisive steppingstone towards general, planet-wide federalization.

[246] In other words, observed on the ground, the escalation and then reversal that occurred in US foreign policy awakened vast repressed local human energies. But their intelligent management would have required a shared learning process, in the absence of which the remedy (at least temporarily) may turn out to be worse than the disease. Consider, for example, what happened in Iraq, Libya, Syria, or Afghanistan. Clearly, Clifford Geertz's (1995, 1999) extraordinary lesson on Muslim world has not been taken into consideration (Meldolesi 2016).

and democracy, ended up favoring China and Russia, as well as promoting the resurgence of autocracies and the spread of anti-Western resentment in many developing countries. In some Mediterranean states this development has generated considerable social, political and military instability through repeated local crises that even today have not been fully contained.

In contrast, the surprise came recently from the Russian invasion of Ukraine, which faced fierce armed resistance, including popular resistance,[247] supported by the Western world beyond its wildest expectations.

At the moment it is difficult to say whether this turn of events heralds a defeat of the Russian Federation and an era of relative stability in power relations between the 'Russian world' and the West, which would have important repercussions in the Mediterranean as well. At the same time, however, this is the most favorable hypothesis underlying our reasoning — if only because possibilist policies, of which we shall speak, require a certain stability if they are to be pursued.

What effect could a turnaround like the US's *recentrage* have on the Mediterranean region, I wondered, if it could be intelligently accommodated in an orderly manner, avoiding the tragedies that have occurred elsewhere?

Step three ('private and public rebellion').

Our southern experience has made it abundantly clear that that sound and independent action arising from nonviolent theoretical-practical rebellion is generally possible — both in the exhilarating, uplifting, and brief phase of the unleashing of social tidal waves, and in the much less attractive phase of the protracted ebb. To be convinced of this, you need to hear part (at least) of the long cultural, educational, professional, entrepreneurial, etc., history that has over time taken up so much of our energy (and which is now largely documented).[248]

One relatively recent turning point in any case deserves particular attention. As in many parts of the world, the social diseases of cronyism, corporatism and lawlessness cohabit with an administrative and political system that leaves much to be desired — to the point that in

---

[247] Particularly well-regarded in the Western world, not least because it exalts the heroism of the Ukrainian people (and at the same time allows U.S. and European military personnel to avoid fighting on the front lines and thus suffer no casualties).
[248] A.A. V.V. 2018-22, Meldolesi 2020,2021, and Meldolesi, ed., 2021 and 2022.

one way or another, the disruptive consequences of genuine impulses for change that rise up from society are often squelched (and perhaps traced back to the usual suspects).[249]

This process (observed on numerous occasions), in its relation to key development issues, to employment, legality, democratic empowerment and so on, at every level of the political and administrative system — from the smallest towns to the national government and the European Commission (along with many of their numerous offshoots) — convinced me that an inversion of the private-public relationship would be useful in expediting the process of change.

To be specific, the formation of substantial private, cultural, and economic 'hubs' of public interest — such as the Harmonic Innovation Group and the Colorni-Hirschman Institute in which my friends and I are currently involved — could encourage the best people in the administration and political system to fine-tune their work and perhaps more robustly nudge the departments they report to along the path of desired change.

Step Four ('civilizing' processes)

So what, then, is the 'object of the exercise'? It is not simply a matter of recognizing the plurality of past and present civilizations, but of realizing that they have differing rates of variation — that is, of becoming civilized.[250] The potential for transformation is often much higher than one might think. It has its roots in the recent and distant history of different places[251] and can be stimulated with appropriate private and public innovations and policies. The possibility of change lies in the actual *pride* that exists in the various communities, and in their struggle against the obstacles, real or assumed, that slow its progress.[252]

---

[249] I speak here with full knowledge of the facts after having observed the actions of numerous friends and collaborators in various positions in the southern administrative and political system and having worked myself for a dozen years in government (and also in Brussels, occasionally) as an advisor and as chairman of the Committee for the Irregular Work Surfacing.

[250] This way of looking at the question moves the focus of the analysis from the relative levels of different civilizations (always debatable) to rates of variation. Because in our time it is possible to set in motion accelerated processes of change with different starting points and multiple consequences, both internal and external. Cf. Lepenies 2013, 279-81 (for the 'civilizations'), and Meldolesi 2013a (for Cattaneo and 'civilizing').

[251] In this regard, the central Mediterranean, with its many generative ancestries (Phoenician-Punic, Magna-Greek, Etruscan, Italic, Gallic, etc.) appears particularly suited to the need.

[252] "Our southern development economics," I wrote recently (2022, 25), "must not lead to a kind of 'doing what everybody does' — because *it cannot,* having cultural, historical and social

It is a great battle that for many areas of the world is not only important in itself, because of the consequences it produces in their local communities — it is also significant for the surrounding areas and for those beyond.

This is a great (misunderstood) lesson of the fall of the Berlin Wall. It is the "magnet effect," which goes beyond individual migrations, and involves entire countries.[253] Furthermore, it can be consciously fostered by building appropriate cultural, economic, and social 'bridges' by strengthening numerous forms of cooperation and exchange.

But those on the other shore who are rebelling for change also need to learn how to do it — get what I'm saying? For example, by shutting the door on any form of violence and staying away from the many gray zones where terrorism is protected (be it religious or otherwise). Many reversals of otherwise valid processes can be traced to such 'deficiencies.' The Muslim Brotherhood and the Arab Spring come to mind.

Step Five ('responsibility and ambition')
Completely accepting the responsibility that all this brings with it and cultivating the greatest of all ambitions — to gradually shrink the global human pyramid in all its many facets, within a framework of freedom, empowerment, and democratization. This is the (temporary) end point of our reasoning.

For this purpose, it is necessary to start moving out into the open — gradually escaping from what we called in the first chapter the 'spiral' of alternating nationalism and imperialism.

Indeed, it is here that, starting small, Mediterranean initiatives with a link to ancient wisdom can play an important role. In his third letter to a German friend, Albert Camus spoke of the "twenty centuries" of the European spirit to be safeguarded against Nazi fury. But now it must be added that the ambition to *move beyond* some of the lessons those centuries have brought with them must also be cultivated.[254]

---

foundations that are different from the richer countries, and because *this is not its intention*. It aims at an alternative civilization, well rooted in traditional behaviors, potentially higher, enabled by the revival of its solid foundations but with the innovative capacities of the present, and capable of ultimately serving the liberating function of the famous Colornian magnet...".
[253] Of course, the process of attraction mainly affects communities that think *(mutatis mutandis)* they can do just as well as what they see happening next door.
[254] Europe "is for us that land of the spirit in which for twenty centuries the most astonishing

And to have a good idea of what this is all about it is in my opinion useful to repeatedly question the era that preceded those twenty centuries. Because I do not believe with Fernand Braudel[255] that the protofederalist period of archaic city-states was fatally destined to succumb to what was ushered in by the great Roman conquests. In my view, rather, at least as far as I can tell, not even the most distinguished exponents of the Phoenician, Magna-Greek, and Italic city-states actually realized that it was their own 'eagerness to dominate' (and to subordinate others) that was 'digging the grave' of that extraordinary experience.

III

6 — Throughout this time, countless human attempts have been made to put feelings of solidarity, fraternity, and equality into practice alongside those for freedom. But the point is that they have never effectively managed to prevail over those of hegemony and domination.[256] They have not succeeded either in international bodies or in the federalist proposals, however attractive, that have been put into practice at different levels.

Whichever way you look at it, the question thus remains open and needs to be relentlessly re-stated,[257] even starting with basic Mediterranean 'solar thinking,' able to correct precisely that 'everybody does it' attitude that prevails in the stagnant mists of other latitudes.

All this will help explain the methodology that was used in composing these pages. That is to say — the texts discussed, the eras sur-

---

adventure of the human spirit has been pursued" (Camus 1962, iv 397-99; cf. above, the opening of Ch. 4). Today those twenty centuries appear to us as a 'double-faced Janus' — a precious legacy and at the same time the living manifestation of an enormous European and world problem still unresolved.

[255] Cf. above, n. 145 and 146. "Braudel explained (1998, 300), among other things, that 'the subjection of Greece to the Macedonian yoke was a consequence of the very expansion of Greek civilization.' Some of the northern regions 'had forged ahead in the fourth century B.C.,' and Macedonia 'eventually took the lead. This was logical enough, since the malaise of the Greek city-states had created — as could also be said of fifteenth-century Italy — a cyclonic zone of low pressure, into which currents were drawn from all sides.' Alexander the Great burst into this void like a meteor, while in our Peninsula the advance of Rome had begun." (Meldolesi 2006, 80-1).

[256] To the point that, for some time now, "antenne 2," the flagship of French television, has been opening its programs with "liberté," "egalité" and ... "actualité"!

[257] The choice is between enslaving domination and moving forward together — between those who presume to impose themselves to the detriment of others and those who, in advancing, are also concerned about those behind them, preferring to reduce distances instead of increasing them — in small things as well as large. Practicing, perhaps without knowing it, the method of affect.

veyed, and the negative turning points on which our attention has been focused (as if it were a generalization of Albert Hirschman's famous "hiding hand").[258]

The truth is, "la pensée de midi" and the Colorni-Hirschman approach are offspring of an era of 'iron and fire.' They emerged in opposition to the foretold tragedy that exploded into World War II thanks to a few extraordinary figures who reacted by putting to use the remarkable abilities they initially did not even know they possessed.

It is also true that other negative turns — such as 9/11 and the Russian invasion of Ukraine[259] — have sorely tested yours truly. But the deeper meaning of the entire line of argument is captured in the Punic Wars, in the clash between Carthage and Rome — at the turning point, that is, between the age of city-states and the now bi-millennial age of nationalism-imperialism.

Perhaps instinctively, Gabriel Audisio got more right than he thought he did, and to convince myself of this, I had to 'rehash' the whole Braudelian question of the discovery of "an America in antiquity." In other words, in order to make sense of the more than 'twenty centuries' that followed the Punic Wars and to *imagine* a future that was 'off the grid' and at the same time loosely interwoven with so much history, it was necessary to make use of a starting point. Also, from the same source *(dulcis in fundo)* an ancient 'legacy' of great value has emerged in the central Mediterranean that could facilitate the development of coming events along unexpected and desired paths. More on this later.

7 — With this, however, we have only set the stage for a discussion of the great problems of humanity that we started with.

Naturally, in order to change things, a conscious (individual and collective) rebellion against injustice is needed — protracted, mature, self-sustaining, committed to cutting-edge economic and social achievements, and open to the positive contributions of the political-administrative system and every other associated dimension (psychological,

---

[258] Hirschman 1967, Ch. 1. Cf. above, Ch. 1, n. 19.
[259] Which, amid much reflection, has forced me to question again the true nature of the regimes which eventually emerged from the great communist revolutions of the 20th century, and more generally the growing danger of autocratic regimes challenging the civil and democratic advances of the liberal revolutions (and the Paris Commune). Here again we get a glimpse of a negative turn in the human adventure, which could, however, trigger a massive new liberating reaction...

scientific, artistic-cultural, etc.) of daily life.

What is needed is a (Colornian) rebellion that is "at once a critic and a linchpin" such as will allow the energy that is mobilized to achieve the desired results — a long-term rebellion that must first and foremost be defended against those who might harm it (whether in the public or private system, and whether inside or outside the reality progressively coming under consideration).[260] It can and must flourish within the constellation of circumstances, on the whole complicated, but (it must be added) by no means prohibitive, in which we typically find ourselves operating.

To explain myself better I will return briefly to the five steps set out above.

In the first place, what can we say after so many years about Colorni's visionary thesis about the process of constructing European unity and the beneficial influence that it could exert internationally? In effect, partial and circuitous as it is, just such a positive trend began to occur. Just think of the fall of the Berlin Wall, the collapse of the USSR and real European socialism.

But I hasten to add, all that turned out not to be enough. It was not understood, and its extraordinary potential was possibly not even sensed. There was no intelligent accommodation when such a thing would have been possible — transforming Gorbachev's openness to the West into a possible European political-democratic haven grounded in the great Russian culture of the past.[261]

In other words, the Colornian ideas of European unity and the civilizing process as a magnet have proven their worth. They have been intrinsic to events of great historical importance such as those just mentioned. Yet the mistakes made by the EU and the US at such junctures were so egregious that even long after the event, we are still paying dearly for them.[262]

---

[260] Paraphrasing Hirschman (1995, p.299-300; cf. below, n. 270), it can be argued in this regard that, in order to fulfill their promises to their own citizens and to humanity as a whole, democratic societies need "a steady diet of rebellion." For this sets them in motion toward their desired goals and at the same time indirectly legitimizes their own functioning.

[261] Indeed, at that juncture, the disappointment produced by Western obtuseness and the downgrading (painfully perceived as dishonorable) that followed it sadly pushed the Russian Federation down the road of revenge — that is, toward Yeltsin, and then to Putin's long reign. Hence the great Russkiy Mir (Russian world) project, based on an eternal core of values, traditions and religion antithetical to that of the West — the basis of a new, dangerous, and potentially planetary belligerent challenge.

[262] It is enough to note that in thirty years, the established democracies (US in the lead) have

Nevertheless, the appeal of the EU has not been extinguished. "The magnetism exerted by Europe," Maurizio Ferrera (Ferrera, 2022) has written, "has much to do with hopes for economic prosperity. But most of the former Soviet republics are also interested in two kinds of guarantees. Security from external threats, first and foremost [...]. And secondly, freedom and tolerance — they wish to be able to enjoy the civil rights that are instead despised and often mocked by Russian leaders and Orthodox hierarchies."

Hence, then, the Western reaction to the barbaric invasion of Ukraine: the enlargement and strengthening of NATO; the EU opening to Ukraine, Moldova, and Georgia, then Albania and northern Macedonia; the foreseeable
consequences for the other Balkan states on the waiting list; and the hope that this will also lead to indispensable reforms in the EU itself.

8 — Of course we cannot know whether in future months the solid political, economic and military support of the West will be enough to ensure that David, however courageous and determined, is not in the end suffocated by Goliath in the terrible, ruthless war of systematic destruction that we have unfortunately come to know.[263] But one fact is certain — the appeal of the democratic world exists and is reproduced on and off with respect to Eastern Europe. We also need to know how to direct it to the Russian people in the east and to the Muslim world in the south.

It seems to me, on the other hand, that in some of Colorni's later decisions (which many have too hastily considered as personally motivated) there is a perception of "thought from the meridian" about to blossom. And this impression is better understood after a reading of Albert Camus's *The Rebel*.

This is to say that the Melfi experience (corroborated by the Four Days of Naples) convinced Eugenio that he needed to commit himself fully to building the Roman Federalist movement and then launching

---

been able to turn the vain and unhealthy euphoria of the so-called "end of history" into a very serious resurgence of autocracies worldwide.

[263] At this moment, we can only list some major consequences of the dreadful upheaval — the destruction and the human tragedies that the invasion has generated; the sanctions and the war effort; the respective hardening of the warring sides and their allies; the looming danger of further widening of the conflict; the formation of blocs and sub-blocs of countries aligned on either side and the changing political, economic and military power relations with in them; energy and food crises and their devastating consequences; inflation; the emergence of vast intermediate zones determined to make then way between the two camps...

the Resistance against the invader, which would later victoriously spill over into the north-central part of the country.[264] So that it was a "wind from the south" that was already blowing and would bring decidedly beneficial effects (however misunderstood) to all of Italy — to win the war, first and foremost,[265] but also to contribute to the commencement of the European and world federalism that Colorni had envisioned at Ventotene (in his well-known critical dialogues with Ursula Hirschmann, Altiero Spinelli and Ernesto Rossi).

IV

9 — Under conditions of democracy, Colornian politics is obviously peaceful and pacifist, in the sense that it requires peace and the peaceful and democratic influence of the people on institutions and thus political choices. It calls for an intelligent and resourceful capacity for rebellion against injustice (but respectful of institutions), uncommon initiative skills on the part of stakeholders, peaceful opportunities (even when unexpected), and even glimpses of new shared pacifist horizons.

Despite the many swings and pirouettes of the new international order, something like this actually got started (albeit piecemeal) in the 1950s.[266] It had as its premise the victory in World War II, reconstruction via the Marshall Plan, the defeat of reactionary ideologies a la McCarthy, the political stability of armed peace (the Cold War)... and also concern for the human condition in general (developing peoples included)[267] — not least dictated (*ça va sans dire*) by Western geo-strategic interests.

In practical terms, Colornian politics aims to condition the fluctuating political currents of the great powers and their allies in such a way that the will of the people pushes them to reflect the genuine demands of women and men of every circumstance, excluding none, exploiting every form of peaceful expression.

---

[264] Rather than joining the Spinelli-Rossi leadership of the Federalist Movement in Switzerland.
[265] On this point I recall Hirschman's (1987, 41) assertion that until Hitler's defeat his every thought of sought a way to connect with that purpose.
[266] As Vittorio Coda said after reading a key page of Colorni's (2019a, 160-62): "that's what happened."
[267] All this better explains Colorni's final itinerary and Hirschman's initial one: the antifascist struggle, the participation in the Marshall Plan, the decision to work in Bogotá... In addition, the reader will already have noted a possible comparison with the present set up — the need to end the Russian invasion, to rebuild Ukraine and to stabilize the overall situation — probably under another armed peace...

Moreover, in order to strengthen its influence, it can build, even in less privileged areas, prototypes (or examples) of civilizing processes with notable appeal to the surrounding populations. This is the policy of the magnet, according to which, by successfully achieving economic (and any other) results far superior to current ones, one indirectly stimulates initiative in others.[268]

10 — Inevitably, what I am trying to construct does not fit with economic (or other social science) models that claim to be applicable *sic et simpliciter,* following their own tortuous mechanical (or 'mechanistic') logic. It must be adapted, case by case, to concrete situations, and it must be corrected and made to evolve in dialogue with actual experience, with life as it is lived.

Every stretch of road that leads to any degree of success needs to be broken down and reassembled so that useful lessons can be drawn from it. This is not least because what is intended needs to adapt itself to the existing constellation of circumstances and its evolution. Consider, for example, social tides, their emergence, their knock-on effects, explosion, and then ebbing. A Colornian-Hirschmanian political approach cannot do other than link itself to the great energy these give off, with a view of consciously turning them to constructive ends.

Policies of well-functioning federalist democracy, prosperity, liberty, social justice, environment, education, health care, etc., are an excellent drawing card for those who enjoy such blessings only partially (or not at all) and they in fact suggest to these people significant changes in their options.

This means then that when favorable conditions arise, attempting to intentionally reproduce the desired path becomes interesting, perhaps involving embarking on (or inventing) a new road among a thousand possible ones, and by bringing in other consenting parties (with the utmost respect for their independence).

11 — Of course, we must not underestimate the difficulties. With this in mind — just to be clear — I want to borrow a leading idea of Camus's in *The Rebel,* according to which rebellion and homicide are antithetical forms of behavior. This is a crucial question, especially when we are trying to imagine the applicability of Colornian-Hirschmanian

---

[268] This is an essential part of the truly surprising and unexpected social mechanism that eventually led to the fall of the Berlin Wall and its many spectacular consequences.

politics to other periods or areas in the Mediterranean. For example, the Arab Spring risings were genuine rebellions on the part of many thousands of young people, but were sadly marred by the fact that Camus's basic truth had not been learned in time — to the point that the events are commonly remembered today almost backwards, as birds of ill omen, the inadvertent heralds of multiple tragedies...[269]

At this point, I would expect a certain outcry from those who, in the course of their own rebellions (political, social, cultural, artistic) have experienced (or heard about) some of the many events I have mentioned. Let me reassure them. My intention is not to judge such events (much less to absolve them retrospectively 'en mass'). I respect the judgment (often critical, more or less overt) that each has given of them and that it has "something to do" with earlier uprisings (why else would the latter have occurred?). I only mean to suggest mildly that, however things played out in specific detail, certain postwar events (concerning stabilization, economic growth, the functioning of democratic systems, the start of the European Community) — the consequences of so many battles[270] — ended up creating the conditions conducive to the collective processes that resulted finally in the fall of the Berlin Wall and its extraordinary consequences.

---

[269] However, such dismissive judgments are external to the realities under discussion, probably unfair, and at best reflect the disappointment of those who, starting under their own conditions, often very different, would have wished for different results. Quite different judgments would probably be reached by someone in a position to 'drop' into the current social processes and their development. The general impression is that, at this time, Islamist-motivated terrorism has lost some of its explosive momentum in its spread over a much wider area (from the Middle East to the Horn of Africa, the Sahel, northern Nigeria, etc.). It appears that territorial struggles, which are very widespread, currently have a more contained degree of violence — possibly a sign of a process of self-reflection which has nevertheless not yet managed to emerge with the necessary vigor. This seems to favor (unfortunately) the expansion of a large area (even if only formally) in connivance with the siren of terrorism. Conclusion — this situation still prevents the creation of tendentially egalitarian relations. It is essential to be totally explicit on this point.

[270] "In societies with freedom of speech and association, concerns about those matters [social, sectoral or regional inequalities] tend to mobilize the people who are immediately affected as well as citizens who are sensitive to more or less widely shared feelings about social justice. These two groups make demands for corrective action and reform [...]. Tire secret of the vitality of pluralist market society and of its ability to renew itself may lie in this conjunction [of private interests and concern for public welfare] and in the successive eruption of problems and crises. The society thus produces *a steady diet of conflicts* that need to be addressed and that the society learns to manage."

V

12 — To see how this works in the case of the Mediterranean — this is my argument — Colornian-Hirschmanian readers and their Audisian-Camusian counterparts must in a certain sense *rise above* their respective ways of thinking. This is true of the former, because even to gain access to a more artistic and perceptive horizon they must explicitly insert the idea of the "wind from the south" into their reasoning, along with that of the opposition between rebellion and violence. And the latter because they simply cannot stop at the threshold of the social sciences if they are to understand and put into practice the idea (which seems inevitable to me) that without economics (politics, sociology, anthropology, psychology, etc.) there is simply 'no game.'

In fact, 'the magnet' has to prove its *superiority* in the processes of civilizing; and this becomes possible only when the effectiveness/efficiency/innovation, adjusted to the local conditions of the stakeholders (and thus their current and potential productivity), is taken into account.

Nevertheless, once such difficulties have been overcome, I believe the dialogue between the two points of view can rapidly lead to a series of mutual benefits. Colornian-Hirschmanian-trained readers will gain easy access a vast Mediterranean inventory of proportion, beauty, pleasantness, *joie de vivre,* lifestyles, environment, nature, etc., which they have always perceived, but which often, caught up in a thousand modernist attractions, they have taken for granted and thus not 'made a sufficient case' for — while on the other hand (and rightly!) the Mediterranean storytellers of the 'Algiers group' and their emulators have never tired of noting its crucial importance.

And the Audisian-Camusian-trained reader who is approaching the world of Albert Hirschman will be better able to appreciate some of the philosophical-political roots of Hirschman's thinking, some of the possible inspirations that can be drawn from it, and possibly further developments as well.

For Audisio, Camus, Colorni, and Hirschman the problem *has always been* to 'go off the grid' in order to substantially correct 'conventional wisdom.' Relentlessly revitalizing their views and aiming for a better world in light of the new conditions remains high on the agenda of the insurgent women and men of our time (and beyond).

13 — And yet by doing this we will have (only partly) come to grips with *one* of the questions that interests us — concerning two minor sister-traditions that have unfolded by fits and starts (so far without interacting) over the last century. I find myself wondering how to enter into dialogue with the others that certainly exist — both in France and Italy and in the rest of the northern (Iberian, Balkan, Greek, Turkish...) side of the Mediterranean.

But most of all, I wonder how to deal with the big issue of meridian thinking with reference to the eastern and southern sides of the Mediterranean. Here I inevitably rim up against the other shock at the origin of the present work — '9/11' and its noxious consequences. I reacted initially by organizing a joint conference with the American Consulate at the Faculty of Economics of the Federico II University in Naples in solidarity with the hard-hit people of the United States.[271] I also sought refuge, as I have mentioned, in the ancient history of the Mediterranean, perhaps in part because I was 'seeking enlightenment' in primitive Phoenician, Etruscan, Magna-Greek, Italic federalism, to be crafted as an alternative to what was happening.

Furthermore, after the resurrection of Islamic terrorism in the form of Isis, I returned to the subject by drawing on the anthropological work of Clifford Geertz, a friend and partner of Albert Hirschman at the Institute for Advanced Study at Princeton, who had spent a lifetime putting significant parts of two countries located at the extremes of the great Islamic arc — Morocco and Indonesia — under the lens of his extraordinary mental microscope. I argued on that occasion for the need to *Mend the World*.[272] In addition, having learned more or less by chance that in antiquity violence had never originated in religion, I undertook to study the genesis of the belligerent historical antagonism between Christianity and Islam — and from there ultimately advocated the (Hirschmanian) denunciation of the rhetoric of intransigence, and supported secular and religious currents opposed to terrorism.[273]

---

[271] Meldolesi 2004, Ch. 1.
[272] Meldolesi 2004, 2006, 2016 and 2018. These and other works still await a retrospective self-subversive adjustment. In fact, all it takes is to begin listing them for me to become aware of the dismay and persistent worry that the attack on the twin towers and then the Isis Caliphate in Iraq and Syria provoked in my mind. The vexed issue of finding suitable solutions for the gradual healing of such serious wounds remains unanswered.
[273] Thus, I went on, in my own way. with the journey begun with *The Game of the Gods* (2006).

14 — They were small successive 'pieces' of an inner drive to find a way out of a troubling situation which — I see it better now than then — was reshaping the world horizon, with the economic rise of China and the growth of Russian military influence that has over the years closely tracked the gradual repositioning of the United States.

Retrospectively, I am glad to note that these works got me (almost involuntarily) to 'dirty my hands' in a major issue — relations with Islam[274] — which undoubtedly goes beyond my current cognitive and operational skills (and the purposes of this work). After all, it is true that, like Spain, Italy has very ancient relations with Semitic (Phoenician- Punic, Jewish and then Muslim) culture — so much so that many parts of the country are influenced by it, even without realizing it, in everyday life (in dialects, attitudes, religious and culinary traditions, etc.). But it is also true that the historical events of the last century, with the ouster of fascism (and Italian colonialism) by popular demand brought as an (unintended) consequence an era of respect for the sovereignty of Muslim countries and peoples, and at the same time practical-psychological remoteness.

In other words, while on Europe's eastern flank the Colornian approach to social change has had an extraordinary and unexpected debut that tends to reproduce itself, and may gradually become more deliberate, on the southern side of the Mediterranean this has not yet occurred.

VI

15 - The magnet effect toward the south and southeast is affecting individuals (and thus immigration[275]) more than populations and their states. The colonial past inevitably weighs heavily and, looking back, military-religious antagonisms and finally the complexity of relations between the Semitic-Muslim and Greco-Roman legacies. The truth is, we have behind us a long history of coexistence, but also one

---

And it does not seem coincidental to me that with a longer historical view, a certain interest in ancient, polytheistic myths is back in vogue today — from the "Path of the Gods" on the Amalfi Coast that meanders past my Agerolese writing desk, to the thousands of B&Bs that have sprung up like mushrooms in its wake, to Guidorizzi and Romani's *La Sicilia degli dèi* [The Sicily of the Gods] (2022).

[274] And are thus situated upstream from the encounter with "la pensée de midi" that is the focus of the present work.

[275] A broad and complex topic (from sea tragedies to reception issues, to European redistribution failures, to social integration, labor, small business, etc.) that is necessarily beyond the scope of this research.

of envy, mutual distrust, and rivalry. In concrete terms, this has in turn weakened the development of effectively representative Mediterranean 'solar thinking' and its influence in the direction of northern Europe (mentioned by Camus) as well as southern Africa and the Middle East.

And so? So, it is useful to invest in 'friendly bridges' of the most diverse nature, and to avoid forcing things. Indeed, it is important to let time take its course. Given present conditions, true intellectual and cultural 'interactions' between the two shores are not currently within our reach. But economic ones exist — consider the willingness of young people, the energy and environmental needs that beset us, and the necessity that 'everyone' focus on innovations in a time of great structural transformation.

What is more, after much searching (and not much finding) in a fluid period marked by terrorism and profound change, we are today experiencing a sort of return to the past — with war in Europe and the formation of opposing blocs. Paradoxically, this facilitates the task we have set ourselves — in the sense that our workhorses from the past, in terms of education, development, employment, administration, territory, independence, and innovation can find new vitality building from within the democratic world and opening up to the left and right.

16 — This is a civilizing spiral and thus one whose appeal may interest the other shore of the Mediterranean — not least because the rapid growth of economic relations between Israel and some Muslim countries may set the stage for a broader trend.

In other words, while we await the emergence — in both the Jewish and Muslim camps — of authoritative and passionate advocates 'for a better world' (and also for promoting its formation) it seems to me important to focus our efforts on the available resources (cultural, political, economic) that exist in the Italic, Magna-Greek and Phoenician heritage of the Italian Mezzogiorno, with a view to radiating out, in every direction, the expected future results, and with the hope of helping to set a favorable process in motion elsewhere as well — a sort of 'one thing leading to another' — toward new goals. To this must be added the ambition of creating over time inter-Mediterranean relations of parity that will strengthen the trend (which already exists internationally) toward moving beyond both rivalries between powers and relations of domination/subordination between people, peoples, and countries.

Naturally, this is easier said than done. First, because 'hegemonic' ideas prevail by far in the multidimensional hierarchies in which, like it or not, we are all enmeshed.

17 — This brings us finally to a *dénouement*. Because at this point the 'Etruscan question' discussed above in the second chapter seems particularly instructive.

As you will recall, "Etruscan rule," according to Carlo Cattaneo (Cattaneo, 1844a; now 1957, 799-800 and 799),[276] had created a *"nursery of cities, a generator of cities"* — "federated and multifaceted, it could tame barbarism without extinguishing independence." The Etruscan League of twelve Tuscan republics had expanded its range of activity to the north into the Po Valley and to the south into Campania, and it "held all points of Italy and the islands, and encompassed with its trade, with its rites, and with its law, the peoples of the aboriginal tribes, in times before the Italo-Greek era."

Later, however, even the Etruscan world (as we mentioned above, chaps. 2 and 3) was gradually dragged into the game of rivalries and power politics that led to its tragic dissolution.

But this does not erase the incontrovertible historical fact of the seven-century prevalence of Etruscan rule in a vast area of Italy (an alternative to Roman rule and the entire nationalist-imperialist tradition).

The surprise, then, is that even after so much time, we can still learn from Etruscan rule and more generally from the federalism that blossomed with the system of city-states (Italic, Phoenician, Magna-Greek, Greek).[277]

Not because we can revive their exploits. But rather, because, while acting from within, from one part — the Western democratic part — of the national-imperial system that rules the world today, we have the audacity to work against the grain armed only with the Colornian policy of the civilizing magnet.

We mean to fight backwardness by promoting independence in a federating-democratic framework, expanding liberty along with equa-

---

[276] Cf. above, secs. 3 and 17 of Ch. 2.
[277] Learn as a starting point, but also as an endpoint. In fact — and I will make this clear on another occasion — the study of so many contemporary versions of federalism (including those that arose historically out of the American Revolution) has ultimately led me to the conclusion that, however useful and appealing they may be in practice in today's world, they are not capable, as such, of effectively countering current relations of domination/subordination.

lity and fraternity, and reducing (instead of extending) the multidimensional domination/subordination pyramids of which we now find ourselves a part.

It is in fact true that apart from the very top and bottom, each of us feels 'prima facie' subordinate to others and in turn a subordinator of still others. As a result, we dream of moving up on the ladder, reducing our subordination and ... expanding our dominion.

This is hard to pin down, and in fact we need to keep the two issues separate. It is perfectly possible to elevate oneself (and, at least in part, to have this recognized) without thereby imposing one's dominance on others — being able rather to 'lend a hand' to those who follow in order to build relationships with them that tend to be equal.

It thus becomes clear that the progressive reduction of inequality is a goal to be pursued relentlessly, by fighting against the opposite trend and repositioning oneself accordingly in thought and action — both personally and collectively. This not least because anyone who doesn't find the strength to behave coherently on this point will easily (and unconsciously) fall back into dominance-related behavior.[278]

---

[278] There is one last topic that I can only mention. There is an increasingly influential presence of "Italic" and "Mediterranean" individuals in many corners of the interconnected world who might over time take on a role of mediation and conflict mitigation, with positive spillover effects even in our own neighborhood.

Bibliography

A.A. V.V. (1988) *I Fenici*, Milano, Bompiani.
A.A. V.V. (1996) *I Greci in Occidente*, Milano, Bompiani.
A.A. V.V. (2000) *Gli Etruschi*, Milano, Bompiani.
A.A. V.V: (2013) *Le noir et le bleu. En rêve méditerranéen...*, Marseille, MuCEM.
A.A. V.V. (2018-22) *Italia Vulcanica.*, Fascicoli 1-13, L. Meldolesi ed., Roma, Ide...
AA. V.V. (2020) "Montagne russe". *Italia Vulcanica n. 6-7*, L. Meldolesi ed. Roma, Ide....
Agostino, A. St. (397-400; 1992 f.) *Confessioni*, Milano, Valla-Mondadori; English trans. Cambridge, MA, Harvard UP, 2014.
Agostino, A. St. (426; 1997) *Citta di Dio*, Roma, Citta Nuova; English trans. New York, New City P, 2012.
Andreae, B. (2004) "La tomba François ricostruita," in A.M. Moretti Sgubini ed., *Eroi etruschi e miti greci, gli affreschi della tomba François tornano a Vulci*, Vulci, Eca.
Audisio, G. (1935) *Jeunesse de la Méditerranée I*, Paris, Gallimard.
Audisio, G. (1936) *Jeunesse de la Méditerranée II, Sel de la mer*, Paris, Gallimard.
Audisio, G. (1946) *Ulysse ou l'intelligence*, Paris, Gallimard.
Audisio, G. (1954) "Le génie de l'Afrique du Nord de Saint Agustin a Albert Camus," *Annales du Centre universitaire méditerranéen*, 7e vol., 1953-54.
Audisio, G. (1960) "L'Algerien," *La nouvelle Revue Française*, Hommage à Albert Camus 1913-1960, Paris, 1° mars.
Benoît, F. (1931) *L'Afrique méditerranéenne*, Paris, Les Beaux- Arts.
Berque, J. (1998) *Une cause jamais perdue. Pour une Méditerranée plurielle. Ecrits politiques 1956-1995*, Paris, Albin Michel.
Bondì, S. F. (2003) "La colonizzazione fenicia," *Archeo*, n. 2.
Bourdet, C. (1975) *L'aventure incertaine, De la Resistance a la Restauration*," Stock.
Braudel, F. (1981) *La dinamica del capitalismo*, Bologna, Il Mulino.
Braudel, F. (1987) "La storia" in F. Braudel, *Il Mediterraneo*, Milano, Bompiani
Braudel, F. (1998) *Memorie del Mediterraneo*, Milano, Bompiani.
Cambiano, G. (2022) *Filosofia greca e identità dell'Occidente*, Bologna, Il Mulino.

Camus, A. (1937) "La culture indigène. La nouvelle culture méditerranéenne," *Jeune Méditerranée*, Alger.
Camus, A. (1939) "Misère de la Kabylie" *Actuelles*, iii, 1958 cit.
Camus, A. (1942) *L'Etranger*, Paris, Gallimard.
Camus, A. (1943-44) "Lettres à un ami allemand," *Oeuvres* vol iv, 1962, cit.
Camus, A. (1944) *Caligula*, Paris, Gallimard.
Camus, A. (1945) "Crise en Algérie," *Actuelles*, iii. 1958 cit.
Camus, A. (1947) *La Peste*, Paris, Gallimard.
Camus, A. (1948) "L'exil d'Helene," *Oeuvres* vol. ii, 1962, cit.
Camus, A. (1950) "Noces," *Oeuvres* vol. ii, 1962, cit.
Camus, A. (1951) *L'homme révolté*, Paris, Gallimard.
Camus, A. (1954) "L'été," *Oeuvres* vol. ii, 1962, cit.
Camus, A. (1955) "Lettre à en militant algérien," *Actuelles*, iii. 1958 cit.
Camus, A. (1955-56) "L'Algérie déchire," *Actuelles*, iii. 1958 cit.
Camus, A. (1956) Appel pour une trêve civile," *Actuelles*, iii. 1958 cit.
Camus, A. (1956a) "L'Affaire Maisonseul" *Actuelles*, iii. 1958 cit.
Camus, A. (1958) *Actuelles*, iii. *Chronique algérienne. 1939-1858*, Paris, Gallimard.
Camus, A. (1958a) "Algérie," *Actuelles*, iii. 1958 cit.
Camus, A. (1962) *Oeuvres complètes*, vol. i - vi, Paris, Imprimerie nationale.
Camus, A. Char R. (2007) *Correspondance 1946-1959*, Paris, Gallimard.
Cassano, F. (1996) *Il pensiero meridiano*, Bari-Roma, Laterza.
Cattaneo, C. (1841a) "Della Sardegna antica e moderna," *Il Politecnico*, iv; now in Cattaneo C., *Scritti filosofici* cit. 1957.
Cattaneo, C. (1841b) "Sul principio storico delle lingue europee," *Il Politecnico*, xxiv; now in Cattaneo C., *Scritti filosofici* cit. 1957.
Cattaneo, C. (1844a) "Introduzione" a Cattaneo C, ed., *Notizie naturali e civili su la Lombardia*, Milano, Bernardoni.
Cattaneo, C. (1845) "Dell'India antica e moderna," *Rivista Europea*, Milano (with the title "Sull'imperio indo-britannico"); now in Cattaneo, C. *India, Messico, Cina*. Milano, Bompiani, 1942.
Cattaneo, C. (1861a) "Del pensiero come principio d'economia pubblica," *Il Politecnico* vol. xi; now Milano, Scheiwiller, 2001.
Cattaneo, C. (1861b) "Prefazione" a *Il Politecnico* vol. xi; now in C. Cattaneo, *Storia universale e ideologia delle genti. Scritti 1852-1864*, D. Castelnuovo ed. Torino, Einaudi, 1972.
Cattaneo, C. (1957) *Scritti filosofici, letterari e vari*, F. Alessio ed.,

Firenze, Sansoni.
Charle-Roux, F. (1932) *France et Afrique du Nord avant 1830*, Paris, Alcan
Colorni, E. (1931) "Utilità e moralità nella filosofia politica di Tommaso Campanella," *Rivista di filosofia*, XXII, 3; English trans. in Colorni, *Art* 2022 cit.
Colorni, E. (1998) *Il coraggio dell'innocenza*, L. Meldolesi, ed., Napoli, La Citta del Sole.
Colorni, E. (2019) *The Discovery of the Possible. Excerpts from Political Writings and Correspondence I*, L. Meldolesi and N. Stame eds., New York, Bordighera.
Colorni, E. (2019a) *The Discovery of the Possible. Excerpts from Political Writings and Correspondence II*, L. Meldolesi and N. Stame eds., New York, Bordighera.
Colorni, E. (2021) *'The Philosophical Illness' and Other Writings*. L. Meldolesi, ed., New York, Bordighera.
Colorni, E. (2022) *Art, Aesthetics, Politics*, L. Meldolesi and M. Quaranta eds., New York, Bordighera.
Colorni, E. and Spinelli A. (2020) *Dialogues*, L. Meldolesi ed., New York, Bordighera.
De Sensi Sestito, G. (1988) "La Calabria in età arcaica e classica: storia, economia, società," G. Cingari, ed., *Storia della Calabria antica*, vol. 2, Reggio Calabria, Gangemi.
Domenici, V. (2003) "L'elmo della vittoria tornerà in Italia," *Corriere della Sera*, 10 January.
Fabre, T. (2007) *Eloge de la pensée de midi*, Arles, Actes Sud.
Ferrera, M. (2022) "L'errore di Putin. L'identità più forte dell'Unione Europea," *Corriere della Sera*, 5 July.
Foxlee, N. (2010) *Albert Camus's "The New Mediterranean Culture": A Text and Its Contexts*, Bern, Peter Lang.
François, A. (1857) "Scavi Vulcenti," *Bollettino dell'Istituto di Corrispondenza Archeologica*, p. 97-104.
Frau, S. (2002) *Le Colonne d'Ercole. Un'inchiesta*, Roma, Nur Neon.
Fry, V. (1945,1968) *Assigment: Rescue. An Autobiography*, New York, Scholastic.
Geertz, C. (1995) *Oltre i fatti. Due paesi, quattro decenni, un antropologo*, Bologna, Il Mulino.
Geertz, C. (1999) *Mondo globale, mondi locali. Cultura e politico, alia fine del $xx°$ secolo*, Bologna, Il Mulino.

Grenier, J. (1933) *Les Iles*, Paris, Gallimard ; nouvelle édition, Préface d'Albert Camus, 1959, Paris, Gallimard.

Grenier, J. (1961) *Absolu et choix*, Paris, Presses Universitaires de France.

Grenier, R. (1987) *Albert Camus soleil et ombre. Une biographie intellectuelle*, Paris, Gallimard.

Guidorizzi, G. e Romani S. (2022) *La Sicilia degli dèi. Una guida mitologica*, Milano, R. Cortina.

Guzzo, P. G. (1988) "L'archeologia delle colonie arcaiche," in G. Cingari ed., *Storia della Calabria antica*, Vol. 1, Reggio Calabria, Gangemi.

Guzzo, P. G. (2000) "L'archeologia dei Brettii tra evidenza e tradizione letteraria," in A. Placanica ed., *Storia della Calabria antica*, vol. 2, Reggio Calabria, Gangemi.

Hartz, L. (1955), *The Liberal Tradition in America: An Interpretation of American Political Thought since the Revolution*, New York, Harcourt.

Herubel, M.A. (1928) *L'évolution de la pèche*, Paris, Société d'Editions géographique, maritimes et coloniales.

Hirschman, A.O. (1958) *The Strategy of Economic Development*, New Haven, Conn., Yale UP.

Hirschman A.O. (1967) *Development Projects Observed*, Washington D.C., Brookings.

Hirschman A.O. (1986) *Rival Views of Market Societies and Other Recent Essays*, New York, Viking.

Hirschman, A.O. (1987) *Potenza nazionale e commercio estero. Gli anni Trenta, l'Italia e la ricostruzione*, P.F. Asso and M. de Cecco, eds., Bologna, Il Mulino.

Hirschman, A.O. (1990) *Come far passare le riforme*, L. Meldolesi, ed., Bologna, Il Mulino; English trans. New York, Peter Lang 2021.

Hirschman, A.O. (1995) *A Propensity to Self-Subversion*, Cambridge, MA, Harvard UP.

Ibn Khaldûn (1377; now 1967) *Prolegomenon. An Introduction to History - The Classic Islamic History of the World*, Princeton N.J., Princeton UP.

Lepenies, W. (1992) *Ascesa e declino degli intellettuali in Europa*, Roma-Bari, Laterza.

Lepenies, W. (2013) "Civilizations," in *Le noir et le bleu*, cit.

Lepenies, W. (2020) *Le pouvoir en Méditerranée. Un rêve français pour*

une autre Europe, Paris, La Maison des sciences de l'homme.
Liverani, M. (1988), *Antico Oriente,* Roma-Bari, Laterza.
Lombardo, M. (2000) "Greci e indigeni in Calabria: aspetti e problemi dei rapporti economici e sociali," in A. Placanica ed., *Storia della Calabria antica,* vol. 2, Reggio Calabria, Gangemi.
Manfredi, V. M. (2004) *I Greci d'Occidente,* Milano, Mondadori.
Meldolesi, L. (1984) "'Economia critica' e 'storia della lunga durata'. Un'introduzione," *Inchiesta,* n. 63-4, June (English trans.: *Review,* New York, IX, 1 -1985).
Meldolesi, L. (1992) "Braudel e tm post-scriptum," *Il Ponte,* n. 10.
Meldolesi, L. (1994) *Alla scoperta del possibile. Il mondo sorprendente di Albert O. Hirschman,* Bologna, il Mulino; English trans.: Notre Dame, Univ, of Notre Dame P, 1995; Spanish trans.: Mexico, Fondo de Cultura Econdmica, 1997.
Meldolesi, L. (2004) *Emersione. Dialogo con Marco Biagi,* Roma, Carocci.
Meldolesi, L. (2006) *Il giuoco degli del. Un'angolazione di politica economica alle radici della storia, dell'identità e del federalismo italiani,* Soveria Mannelli, Rubbettino.
Meldolesi, L. (2007) *La quarta libertà. Come padroneggiare la pubblica amministrazione,* Acireale-Roma, Bonanno.
Meldolesi, L. (2013) *Imparare ad imparare. Saggi di incontro e di passione all'origine di una possibile metamorfosi.* Soveria Mannelli, Rubbettino.
Meldolesi, L. (2013a) *Carlo Cattaneo e lo spirito italiano,* Soveria Mannelli, Rubbettino.
Meldolesi, L. (2016) *Rammendare il mondo,* Soveria Mannelli, Rubbettino
Meldolesi, L. (2018) *Intransigenze, Mediterraneo e democrazia,* Roma, Ide... 2° ed. 2019.
Meldolesi, L. (2020) *Eppur si può! Saggi e istruzioni autobiografiche e filo-possibiliste.* Soveria Mannelli, Rubbettino.
Meldolesi, L. (2021) *Mezzogiorno, con gioia!* Soveria Mannelli, Rubbettino.
Meldolesi, L. (2022) *Alla ricerca si una prospettiva. Alcuni scenari,* Roma, ide…
Meldolesi, L. ed., (2021) *Mezzogiorno. Mezzomondo,* Soveria Mannelli, Rubbettino.
Meldolesi, L. ed., (2022) *Protagonismi mediterranei,* Soveria Mannelli, Rubbettino.

Montanelli, I. (1957), *Storia di Roma,* Milano, Rizzoli.
Moscati, S. (1978) (Comunicazione all'Accademia Nazionale dei Lincei), Roma, *Quaderno* n. 238.
Moscati, S. (1995) *Dove va l'archeologia?* Torino Sei.
Moscati S. (1996) *La bottega del mercante. Artigianato e commercio fenicio lungo le sponde del Mediterraneo,* Torino, Sei.
Moscati, S. (1997) *Così nacque l'Italia. Profili di antichi popoli riscoperti,* Torino, Sei.
Ogilvie, R. M. (1984) *Le origini di Roma,* Bologna, Il Mulino.
Pallottino, M. (1984) *Storia della prima Italia,* Rusconi, Milano.
Peroni, R. (1988) 'La protostoria,' in G. Cingari ed., *Storia della Calabria antica,* vol. 1, Reggio Calabria, Gangemi.
Pontrandolfo, A. (2000) "Etnogenesi e emergenza politica di una comunità italica: i Lucani," in A. Placanica ed., *Storia della Calabria antica,* vol. 2, Reggio Calabria, Gangemi.
Pugliese Carratelli, G. (1996), "Profilo della storia politica dei greci in Occidente," in A.A.V.V., *I Greci in Occidente,* Milano, Bompiani.
Robinow, P. and Sullivan, W.M. eds. (1987) *Interpretive Social Science. A Second Look,* Berkeley, CA, U of California P.
Ross Holloway, R. (1995) *Archeologia della Sicilia antica,* Torino, Sei.
Rosso, C. (2017) "Prefazione" to A. Camus *L'Uomo in rivolta,* Milano, Bompiani.
Rustow, D. (1970) "Transitions to Democracy: Toward a Dynamic Model," *Contemporary Politics,* April.
Scirocco, A. (1990) *L'Italia del Risorgimento,* Bologna, Il Mulino.
Semeraro, G. (2005) *La favola dell'indoeuropeo,* Milano, Bruno Mondadori.
Silone, I. (1965) *Uscita di sicurezza,* Firenze, Vallecchi.
Torelli, M. (1984) *Storia degli etruschi,* Laterza, Roma-Bari.
Vidale, M. and Denti M. (1998) *Magna Grecia,* Milano, Fabbri.
Warmington, B.H. (1968) *Storia di Cartagine,* Torino, Einaudi.
Zwingle, E. (2005) *"Italici: i popoli preromani," National Geographic Italia,* n. 1.
Zwingle, E. (2005a), *"Sulle tracce degli etruschi," National Geographic Italia,* n. 1.

INDEX OF NAMES

Abraham Accords 114
Achilles 81, 85
Aeneas 81, 85
Agamemnon 78, 81
Ajax O. 81
Ajax T. 91
Albright, W.E. 29
Alexander the Great 49, 73, 123
Andreae, B. 79, 81
Amphiaraus 78
Archimedes 85-87
Audisio, G. 9, 11-2, 17, 19-39, 49, 51, 53-57, 66-7, 83, 87, 102-107, 109, 113, 115, 117, 124, 130
Augustus 86

Benoît, F. 21
Bonaparte, N. 76, 112
Bonaparte, L. 76
Bondì, S.F. 45
Botticelli, S. 89
Braudel, F. 11, 29, 36, 38-40, 43-45, 48, 52-4, 57, 59-62, 64-5, 67-71, 73-5, 78, 84, 86, 111, 114-15, 123-24
Braudel, P. 28

Cambiano G. 83, 85
Camillus M. 81
Campanella, T. 100
Camus, A. 9-11, 13, 17-20, 22, 27, 32-35, 37, 84, 91-7, 99-104, 106-110, 114-17, 122-23, 126, 128-30, 133
Cassandra 78
Cassano, F. 10
Cattaneo, C. 11-2, 28, 34-6, 38-42, 50, 62-3, 121, 134
Cavallini P. 81
Cervantes, M. de 98
Charles-Roux F. 21

Charun 91
Chiaravalloti, G. 74
Ciampi, C.A. 53
Cicero, M.T. 78, 85
Cingari, G. 74
Coda, V. 127
Colorni, E. 7-9, 11, 13, 18, 22, 26, 36-7, 54-5, 100, 107-09, 115, 117-19, 121-28, 130, 132, 134

Damocles 21, 96
Darius 71
de Ayala R. 28
Denti M. 58
De Sensi Sestito, G. 74-5
Diodorus 71
Dionysius II 60
Domenici V. 58
Dostoevsky, F. 96

Empedocles 85, 87
Eteocles 81

Fabre, T. 9-10, 17, 22, 111, 113-14
Ferrera, M. 126
Fiorino, M. 5
Foxlee, N. 32
Fra Angelico 81
Francis of Assisi 32
François, A. 76-80
Frau, S. 70
Fry, V. 107

Garibaldi, G. 55, 67
Geertz, C. 11, 111, 117, 119, 131
Gelon 72
Gernet, L. 61
Goethe, J.W. von 23, 83-4
Gorbachev, M. 125
Grenier, J. 19, 20, 22
Grenier, R. 32, 37, 91-2
Guerriero, F. 60

Guidorizzi, G. 86, 132
Guilaine J. 28
Guzzo, P.G. 74-5

Hartz, L. 54
Hector 85
Hegel, G.W.F. 97, 100
Herodotus 48
Hérubel, M.A. 21
Hiero 57-8
Hirschman, A.O. 107-8, 111, 115, 117, 119, 121, 124-5, 127-8, 130-31
Hirschmann, U. 108, 127
Hitler, A. 21, 32, 97, 118, 127
Horace 85

Karamazov, I. 96
Keynes, J.M. 11

Leibniz, G.W. von 117-18
Lepenies, W. 9, 11, 92, 111-12, 121
Louis XVI 97
Liverani, M. 7
Livy T. 67
Lombardo, M. 74-5
Lucian 30
Lucretia 80
Lucretius 85
Luther, M. 35
Lysander 73

Machiavelli, N. 100
Mago, 48
Mameli, G. 67
Manfredi, V.M. 72, 84
Marino, V. 12
Marx, K. 98, 100, 107
Massu, J. 116
Mastarna 80
Mazzini G. 67
Menelaus 85
Molière 98
Montanelli, I. 66, 73, 80

Moscati, S. 34, 46-7, 52, 59, 69-71
Muhammad 114
Mussolini, B. 27, 30, 33, 97

Natuzzi P. 61
Nestor 78
Nietzsche F. 23, 32, 97, 114

Pallottino, M. 40-3, 69-70
Patroclus 81
Pericles 60, 73
Peroni, R. 74-5
Perugino 79
Phoenix 78
Pia, P. 91, 93
Pistoletto, M. 113, 118
Pistorio, P. 61
Pythagoras 59, 85, 87
Placanica, A. 74
Plato 60, 87
Pliny the Elder 24, 34, 67
Polynices 81
Pontrandolfo, A. 74
Porsena 73-4, 78
Pugliese Carratelli, G. 66

Ricardo, D. 11
Rabinow, P. 10
Robinson, J. 11
Romani, S. 86, 132
Ross Holloway, G. 7
Rossi, E. 108, 127
Rouillard, P. 28
Rustow, D. 61

Sade D.A.F., Marquis de 96
Scipio Aemilianus 28, 67,
Seneca 85
Servius Tullius 80-1
Shakespeare, W. 98
Silone I. 18
Sisyphus 78
Solomon 29
Sons of Cain 96

Spinelli, A. 7, 22, 55, 108, 118, 127
Sraffa, P. 11
Stalin, J. 99, 101
Stame, N. 12, 78, 87, 111
Stirner, M. 97
Sullivan, W.M. 10

Tanit 48, 71
Tarquin the Superb 73, 74, 80-1, 111
Typhon 69
Torlonia, A. 76-7
Torelli, M. 7, 62

Valery, P. 32, 106
Van Gogh, V. 98
Vanth 81
Varro, M.T. 70
Vibenna, C. 80-1
Vidale, M. 58
Virgil 85

Warmington, B.H. 29-30, 44-5, 47
Weber-Lehman, C. 79
Winckelmann, J.J. 83-4

Xerxes 71

Yeltsin, B.N. 125

Zeus 58
Zwingle, E. 52, 68

ABOUT THE AUTHOR

LUCA MELDOLESI, born in Rome in 1939, taught at the universities of Rome, Calabria, and Naples. President, A Colorni-Hirschman International Institute. He collaborated with Hirschman on numerous books and articles and has applied Colorni's and Hirschman's point of view in his teaching, grass roots initiatives, and in government on behalf of the Italian South.

www.ingramcontent.com/pod-product-compliance
Lightning Source LLC
Chambersburg PA
CBHW020202090426
42734CB00008B/916